Food of the Italian South

CLARKSON POTTER/
PUBLISHERS
NEW YORK

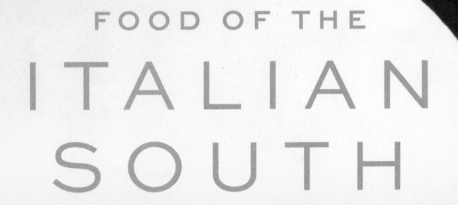

FOOD OF THE
ITALIAN
SOUTH

Recipes for Classic, Disappearing,
and Lost Dishes

KATIE PARLA

PHOTOGRAPHS BY ED ANDERSON

For my sister, Lauren Parla

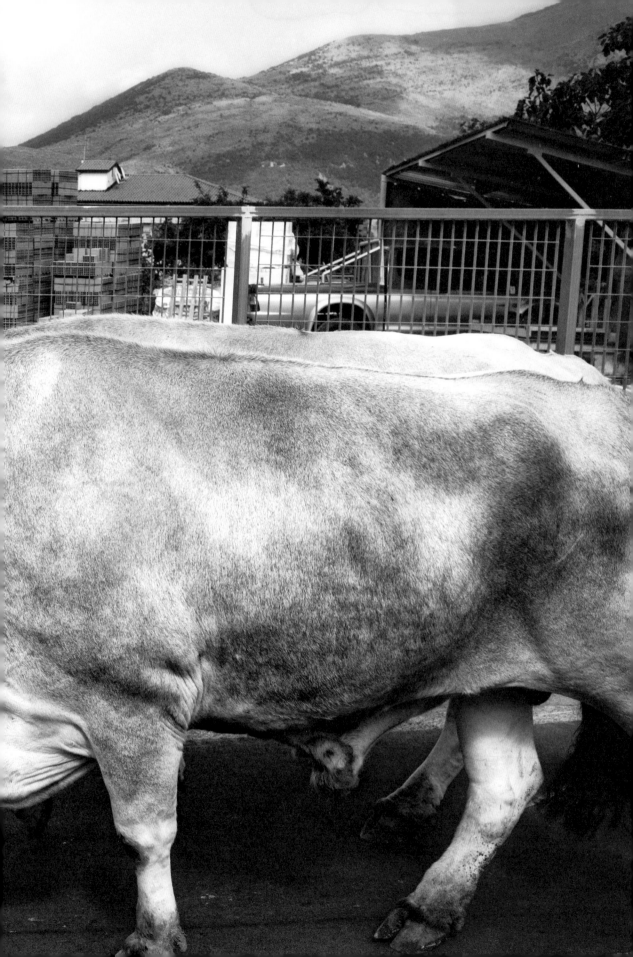

CONTENTS

I was eleven years old when I took my first trip to Italy. It seemed as far away as the moon, and just as foreign. On our first night there, we went to a trattoria for dinner. Some dishes tasted familiar, albeit in much more restrained portion sizes and without the swimming-in-gravy nature of Italian American dishes. But what blew my mind was dessert. At the end of a meal, this native Bronx boy expected cannoli or a big rum cake like at an Italian wedding. What followed, instead, was a come-to-Italian-Jesus moment for me. The waiter brought a giant, weathered pewter bowl. The outside was beaded with sweat, and inside, perfect peaches were bobbing in ice water as though they were swaying on their boughs. With two spoons that seemed extensions of his own hands, the waiter deftly fished in and served us each a perfectly chilled, plump peach. When I bit into it, it didn't taste like any fruit I'd ever had before—I knew that in this moment, I was *really* eating fruit for the first time in my life. Nature had made this thing of infinite perfection and the trattoria knew that the best way to honor this gift was to present it alone, a single ingredient bound to a time and a place.

This restraint, mixed with reverence for nature, is the essence of Katie Parla's *Food of the Italian South*. She carefully lays out the simplicity of the South's cuisine in these pages, at once paying it due respect and elevating it. I knew this woman "got it" from the first moment we met. It was 2016 and I was hosting a dinner to celebrate her first book, *Tasting Rome*, at Tratto, my restaurant in Phoenix. We surveyed the ingredients we'd hauled in that day and chatted about what dessert to serve. As if sharing a brain, we simultaneously decided on the most perfect option before us: fresh, in-season cherries served in ice water.

This affinity for simplicity isn't the only thing I have in common with Katie. Our ancestral paths—not to mention those of millions of other Italian Americans—share many parallels. Many of us grow up with imprecise information about our ancestors. They passed through Castle Garden or Ellis Island, eager to forget the tiny villages and communities of their births and ready to erase their origins in an attempt to assimilate and escape the hardships they were leaving behind in the Old Country. Now, younger generations yearn to know and experience exactly where they came from, which it seems is part of what led Katie to the south.

Food of the Italian South gives us the opportunity to gain perspective in an often overlooked part of Italy in a tactile and human way—Katie artfully guides us through the remote Apennine villages of Campania, the rugged seaside landscapes of Puglia, and the vast grazing lands of Basilicata, delivering their offerings into our kitchens. The whole book is stunning, but her essay on *Frutta*, humble fruit as dessert, spoke to me specifically, triggering the lightning bolt memory of those peaches that helped me gain personal perspective into how I see—and feel—Italian food.

My fascination with the Italian south isn't new. I grew up in an Italian American family in New Jersey, and for as long as I can recall, members of my family have evoked South Italy through expressions they use, dishes they cook, and even (sometimes erroneous) claims they make. My maternal grandmother, Theresa Spisany, always said she was from Naples, so, of course, I always thought we were from Naples. It's the reason that, after moving to Italy in 2003, I kept visiting that sprawling city on a bay. I was convinced it was my ancestral homeland.

As it turns out, we are *not* from Naples. It was just my family's port of departure when they left Italy in the late nineteenth century, shortly after Italian Unification decimated the south's rural economy. But like so many Italian Americans, I only had a vague sense of my origins. We had no reason to doubt my grandmother and no one on her side of the family—especially not her upwardly mobile parents and grandparents— was particularly keen on preserving memories of the impoverished past they had fled. So our false and superficial knowledge of the family history persisted. After my grandmother died, my mom found her family tree in a dresser drawer, sketched on hotel stationery. The branches led back to a town called Spinoso. And just like that, history changed.

I was already living in Italy at the time. My mom flew into Rome to join me on a trip to investigate these newly discovered branches; we rented a car and headed for Spinoso, deep in a remote center of Basilicata, where we found accommodations in one of the town's few rentable rooms. The next day, a trip to the minuscule vital statistics office was fruitful. Three of my grandmother's four grandparents had been born in Spinoso in 1883. Their births had been registered, as had the marriages and births of their parents (thanks, Napoleon, for your legacy of stellar record keeping), so we were able to look at the handwritten documents, which were all kept in enormous fraying leather-bound volumes. Each page was filled with names and dates, recorded in elaborate cursive using sepia ink. As we scrutinized the details, we pieced together a wonderful, if partial, story of my grandmother's family.

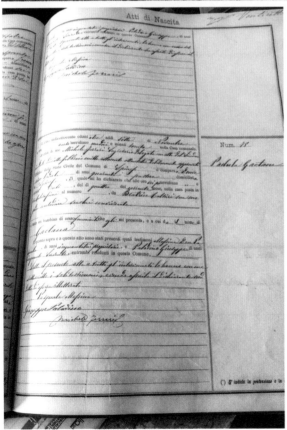

Grandma Theresa was born in Harlem in 1927 to Josephine DeLouise and Francesco "Frank" Spisany. My family doesn't have much information about Josephine's lineage, but Frank's parents were Biase Spisano and Gaetana Padula, who, apparently, were stepbrother and sister. We don't know exactly what year they arrived in America or how Biase's and Gaetana's parents met, but by 1902, they were married with at least one child and living in New York City. Biase was a chauffeur who called himself Biaggo, Will, or William, depending on the day, and affected a British accent to impress his clients. In 1950, Biase "accidentally" shot and killed himself in the family's brownstone in the Bronx.

In Italy, my mom and I tracked down the house where he had been born over a hundred years earlier: a tiny little thing on Gradelle Ecce Homo, a narrow alley behind Spinoso's main church. We didn't find any traces of Biase's older family in any of the town's leather-bound books, but we did learn a lot about Gaetana.

Gaetana was born on Via Calatafimi, a road that runs through the middle of a field, to Beatrice Caltieri, mother of at least six children, the last of whom was born six months after she was widowed. Her male children were all shepherds. Each would receive one small loaf of bread a week as payment for tending a flock, and with these, Beatrice would feed her family.

Gaetana's father, Domenico, died in the house of her birth in 1890 at the age of forty-six. His father, Maurizio Padula, had been a shepherd, as had his grandfather Francescantonio. That's as far back as the records go, but considering that Francescantonio would have been born around 1800, that's seriously impressive by rural Italian standards.

Knowing more about my lineage and the culture and lifestyle from which I come, I better understand my love of South Italy's wide-open pastures, rustic loaves of bread, and grazing sheep. Impoverished shepherds leaving South Italy for the chance at a better life in America may not be a unique story—Biase and Gaetana were just two of the 4 million Italians who emigrated to America as economic refugees in the late nineteenth and early twentieth centuries—but it's *our* story. As it turns out, my devotion to discovering and sharing the rural south is more than just a passion; it's a duty and a tribute to the branches on my family tree.

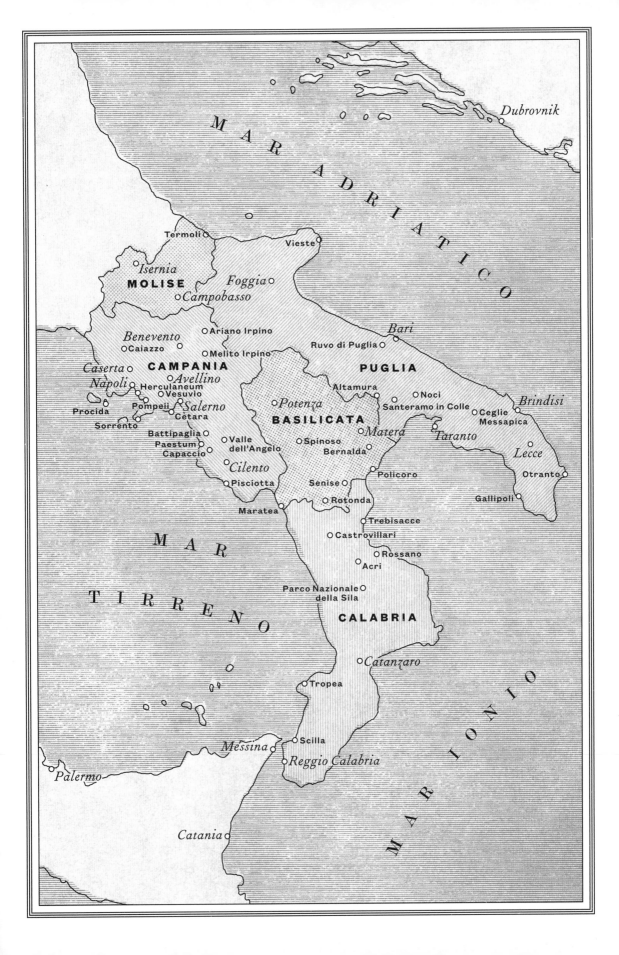

FINDING
THE SOUTH

Before delving into the recipes in this book, familiarize yourself with a map of South Italy (see page 13). We're not exploring "Southern" Italy, which includes the lower peninsula and the islands of Sardinia and Sicily. Rather, we're looking at the south, which is composed of Molise, Campania, Puglia, Basilicata, and Calabria. The Italian statistics bureau and the European Union have made this important differentiation between "South" and "Southern" Italy.

Odds are, if you're Italian American like me, your family is from the south. Some areas get a lot of love in the press (headlines declaring "Puglia Is the New Tuscany" are common) and the Amalfi Coast is world famous, but there are many other spectacular parts of the south that deserve attention. But first, we need to understand the geography of the regions we're discovering in *Food of the Italian South*.

Molise

Molise, southeast of Rome, is a two-hour drive from the Italian capital into the mountainous heart of Italy. The food is hearty, rustic, and vegetable-forward. Until 1970, Molise was part of the combined Abruzzi e Molise region. Now the two regions are separated, making Molise the second smallest in Italy, both by area and by population (first prize goes to Valle D'Aosta). The population has fallen with nearly every census since 1921 due to emigration to Italian cities in the north, as well as to Northern Europe and abroad. The roughly 312,000 *molisani* are mainly clustered around the cities of Campobasso and Isernia, both nestled into the Apennine Mountains. Almost 95 percent of the region is mountainous or hilly, and its sparsely populated land is largely agricultural. Small farms produce *farro* (emmer, spelt, or einkorn, depending on the variety), *cicerchie* (grass peas), and wine grapes like the indigenous Tintilia. The coast of Molise stretches thirty miles along the Adriatic Sea. The main port is Termoli, which is flanked by deserted sandy beaches and the occasional *trabocco*, a traditional wooden fishing platform.

The cuisine is rich in herbs, vegetal soups, lamb, goat, and rabbit. Thanks to their shared geography and history, Molise and its neighbor Abruzzi share many common traditions, such as *ventricina*, a coarse salami flavored with garlic, fennel, and *peperoncino*, as well as some sheep's-milk cheeses. If you're familiar with them, you may notice an *abruzzese* echo in some of the *molisano* recipes here.

Campania

Just south of Molise, Campania is one of Italy's most populated regions, with 5.8 million inhabitants, ranking it behind only Lazio and Lombardy. Dubbed Campania Felix ("fortunate countryside") in Roman times, the region was colonized by Greeks well before Rome arrived and has a millennial tradition of agriculture. The region is known for produce like eggplants, tomatoes, legumes, and peppers, all of which thrive in Campania's nutrient-rich soil.

The region's largest city—and Italy's largest port—is Naples, which sits on a crescent-shaped bay overlooked by Mount Vesuvius and the archeological sites of Pompeii and Herculaneum. The bay is bookended by the wine-producing Phlegraean Fields in the north and the citrus-rich Sorrentine peninsula in the south.

From Sorrento, the jagged Amalfi Coast curves to Salerno, another major port. From there, former marshlands around Paestum, Battipaglia, and Capaccio produce the world's finest buffalo mozzarella. Further south, Cilento's dramatic and sparsely populated coastline rises up to a vast national park, where cows and animals graze through pine forests and across the Vallo di Diano plain. The predominance of fresh fish, seasonal produce, unrefined cereals, and olive oil led the American physiologist Ancel Keys to declare Cilento among the healthiest places in the world. Keys is a champion of the Mediterranean diet, an eating philosophy that posits diet as the main indicator of health and longevity.

The interior of Campania, which is split by the Apennine mountain chain, is divided into a number of subregions. The Alto Casertano near Caserta isn't far from the Molise border and has become a popular destination for pizza tourists, who visit Pepe in Grani to eat Franco Pepe's legendary pies (see page 194) made with local ingredients. The surrounding areas are known for a heritage breed of pig called the Nero Casertano and an ancient style of pungent amphora-fermented cheese called Conciato Romano similar to cave-aged, herb-encrusted sheep's-milk cheeses. The adjacent Sannio area, named for the Samnites, a

bellicose pre-Roman tribe that inhabited the area more than two thousand years ago, is a cluster of remote villages set in the mountainous Parco Regionale del Matese. Just south, Benevento, an ancient city along the Via Appia Antica, is home to Distilleria Liquore Strega (see page 242), the south's most widely distributed liqueur. The steep hills of Irpinia flank Benevento to the northeast, and their dramatic gradients collapse into gentle rolling hills near the Puglia border.

Puglia

When the Mycenaean Greeks landed in Puglia (Apulia in English) in the Iron Age, they found a climate and coastal geography quite similar to their native terrain. Puglia's long coastline wraps around the "heel" of the Italian boot, including the Adriatic along the region's east coast and the Ionian Sea along the west. Stretches of it still have a prehistoric feel thanks to their rocky landscapes. While the major port cities of Taranto and Bari hold commanding positions on the sea, most of Puglia's historically important towns were founded inland to protect against invading fleets and pirates. The western part of the region rises up from the sea to a plateau called the Murgia. This was the breadbasket of ancient Italy, supplying the peninsula with grain. Today, the vast plains of the Murgia grow durum wheat, a main ingredient for the area's rustic breads and hand-shaped pastas.

Basilicata

The Murgia bleeds into Basilicata, among Italy's most mountainous regions, also known by its ancient name, Lucania. The Murgia plateau's durum wheat is milled into flour and baked into rustic loaves in and around Matera, the region's newly rediscovered and reinvigorated troglodyte city and one of several desperately impoverished villages immortalized in writer and activist Carlo Levi's 1945 memoir *Christ Stopped at Eboli*, which details his years in political and intellectual exile under the Fascists. South of Matera and not far from the Ionian Sea, the legacy of ancient Greek colonies survives at Policoro, Italy's strawberry cultivation capital and one of the few stretches of Basilicata's terrain anywhere near sea level. The mountainous interior to the north and east grows potatoes and legumes, while cattle, including the Podolico heritage breed, are raised for their meat and milk.

 The volcanic terrain in the north of the region near the Campanian and Puglian borders grows primarily red grapes, like Aglianico, for wines. The western part of the region has a short coastline along the Tyrrhenian Sea—the main town there is called Maratea. The meager seven-mile stretch means there isn't much fresh fish in the cuisine of Basilicata; the region's fish consumption is mainly *baccalà*, salt cod.

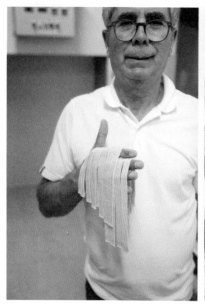

Parco del Pollino, a vast mountainous national park popular with hikers and nature enthusiasts, sprawls over the borders of Basilicata and Calabria. At its southwestern edge around Senise, red peppers are dried and fried. These so-called *peperoni cruschi* are crushed into a powder and used throughout Basilicata to impart a sweet and slightly smoky flavor.

Calabria

Just over the Calabrian border at the edge of the Parco del Pollino, the twisted, mountainous terrain is punctuated with a few dozen villages, home to the Arbëreshë ethnic minority (see page 108), founded in the fifteenth to sixteenth centuries by Albanian refugees fleeing the Ottoman conquest of the Balkans.

Calabria, the "toe" of the boot is a long and mountainous zone known for its pork-driven cuisine. Calabria's geography begets decisive flavors in the form of torpedo-shaped onions from Tropea and piquant licorice from around Rossano. The vast Parco Nazionale della Sila runs through the center of the region and is thick with trees ideal for spawning mushrooms, while the Tyrrhenian and Ionian Seas, which meet at the port city of Reggio Calabria, wrap around the toe and support small-scale fishermen, who catch cuttlefish, swordfish, and tuna in their waters.

UNDERSTANDING
THE SOUTH

"Where is everyone?" It's a question I ask aloud every time I visit the Sannio, Irpinia, Pollino, Cilento, and countless other districts of the Italian south. The simple answer: Like my ancestors, they went to Northern Italy, Northern Europe, or North America to find work. On one hand, the sparse population and lack of mass tourism—and in some areas, lack of *any* tourism—is great, offering quiet and meditative moments that would be fewer and farther between in the densely populated north. But on the other hand, it's a tragedy so many have had to leave and that more visitors haven't yet experienced these regions I love so intensely.

These conditions in the south today were shaped by the unification of Italy in the mid-nineteenth century. King Victor Emanuele II of the House of Savoy and General Garibaldi successfully annexed the large and wealthy Kingdom of the Two Sicilies, an area encompassing modern-day Southern Italy. In order to secure his power and prevent rebellions, the king and Garibaldi introduced policies intended to weaken the south and its economy. First, they broke up or confiscated land from the Catholic Church, an entity that owned a significant percentage of the land in the south. Next, they undermined the land holdings of wealthy families, imposing similar measures to divide and redistribute the territory they owned. In doing so, the unification government looted the south and upset the feudal system of land ownership and labor that had defined the south for centuries, ensuring the survival of its people. Farmers and laborers worked the land of the rich and lived off what they grew. Sure, it was a system that relied on an uneven distribution of wealth, but it provided the basics to the people. This delicate balance was upset after unification, and rural peasants, no longer bound to landholders, faced unemployment and starvation in staggering numbers. Millions of peasants fled to the ports of Bari, Naples, and Reggio Calabria to board ships to America, while others made their way to Italy's rapidly industrializing northern cities: Rome, Milan, and Turin.

The south never rebounded after unification, and over the past century and a half, policies and development strategies crafted in Rome have favored the powerful economic interests in the north. But in spite of it all, the south remains resilient. The ancient, food-driven culture embodies the spirit and atmosphere of this place and its people. By exploring the food here, you're exploring history.

So much of what we know and enjoy as "Italian food" today comes from this place, but we forget to honor and appreciate and understand it. Everyday fare is simple and rustic and relies on seasonal ingredients culled from fertile earth, while holiday meals are elaborate, celebratory expressions with layered flavors and many ingredients that would be easily recognizable to anyone familiar with Italian cuisine. Indeed, the primary ingredients of the south are the very ones that outsiders identify as distinctly Italian: buffalo mozzarella, durum wheat pasta, eggplants, and ripe tomatoes. The dishes are widely beloved, too—whether in a cookbook or on a restaurant menu, you have likely encountered *insalata caprese* (caprese salad) and *parmigiana di melanzane* (eggplant Parm), among other South Italy staples. There are plenty of excellent cookbooks and websites out there that cover these and other classics; some of these are listed in the bibliography on page 247. The ninety recipes in this book include a handful of such well-known items as *Minestra Maritata* (page 74) and *Casatiello* (page 182), as well as some more modern dishes like *Orecchiette con Burrata, Pomodorini, e Pesto* (page 98), but this book's primary focus is to go beyond the flavors and dishes that have migrated across the Atlantic. Each recipe here has been chosen to form part of a portrait of the south, and each has its own story to tell. Some, like *Insalata di Rinforzo* (page 156), are staples across large swaths of the south, while others, like *Manell'* (page 40), are unique to a single remote village. Still others are on the verge of extinction, or have already vanished from tables and exist only as distant memories. I want to spotlight the people, ingredients, and recipes that are so deeply anchored in the Italian south that they haven't had the opportunity to travel very far. Not until now, anyway.

Still today, the south's economic conditions and relative isolation make it a complex but rewarding place to love. It's easy to fall head over heels for Venice's canals. And don't get me wrong, I love Modena's elegance and the Dolomites' gray-blue hues. But I cannot live without the south, its long stretches of rugged beaches, its mountains populated with more sheep and cows than humans, and, above all, its soulful culinary traditions and pure ingredients.

ABOUT THIS BOOK

Organization

The recipes in this book are divided by courses, to reflect the traditional structure of a meal in the south, but you can mix and match dishes in your own kitchen based on the season, occasion, and ingredients you have on hand, or your appetite. The *Antipasti* chapter covers starters served to usher in the beginning of a large weekend meal or holiday feast. *Zuppe e Minestre* covers hearty stews and brothy soups that provide delicious and nutritious ways to consume plentiful seasonal produce and legumes. The *Pasta* chapter includes instructions for making and shaping fresh pasta, as well as recipes made with dried pastas and suggestions on how to perfectly pair condiments with pasta shapes. The *Pesce* and *Carne* chapters deal with *secondi* (mains) made with seafood and meat, respectively. *Contorni* encompass a wide range of side dishes and, like *Zuppe e Minestre*, are a celebration of seasonal produce. The *Pane, Focaccia, e Pizza* chapter is a survey of loaves, flatbreads, and buns you might encounter in a bakery in Bari or Matera and even includes a *pizza napoletana* recipe (page 189) adapted for the home oven. The *Dolci* chapter offers cookies and tarts, and highlights the almonds and spices that pastry lovers in the south crave. Finally, the *Liquori e Cocktail* chapter is filled with herbal and fruit-based digestifs essential for processing dishes from the aforementioned categories.

While these recipes were developed alongside home cooks, chefs, farmers, and bakers in Italy's five southern regions, all were tested in the United States and have been adapted for a home kitchen.

Measurements and Seasoning

I documented recipes of the south in the spirit of rustic cooking, which doesn't get bogged down with precise ingredient amounts or proportions. Flip through any Italian cookbook and you'll find lots of references to a pinch, a handful, or simply "q.b.," meaning *quanto basta*, "as much as you need."

While South Italy's truly authentic recipes might just be a list of ingredients without defining precise quantities, I have written the recipes using US measurements. But feel free to treat most as guidelines that can be adjusted to your personal palate. Do, however, stick closely to the quantities in the baking recipes unless you are an expert baker. I've also listed metric measurements for bread and pizza baking recipes. Please use them! They are more precise than imperial measurements and are key to achieving the most successful results.

When salting water for cooking dried pasta or vegetables, use enough salt so that the water actually tastes salty; 3 tablespoons salt for every 6 quarts water should do it. I don't expect you to actually measure every time, but do it once, taste the water, and aim for that salinity every time. For cooking fresh pastas, the recipe will instruct you to "heavily salt the water," meaning to add more salt than you would for dried pasta. You want the water to be nearly as salty as seawater when you taste it. The reason for this is that fresh pasta only spends about 3 minutes in the water (as opposed to anywhere between 8 and 16 minutes for dried pasta), so it has less time to absorb the salt. Three minutes in very salty water should result in moderately seasoned pasta.

Always read the entire recipe before beginning to cook. Some recipes require prep work in advance, which will be mentioned in the headnote. I almost always recommend salting proteins before cooking them. Salting meat and fish in advance gives the salt time to penetrate and flavor the meat. Tough cuts and whole muscles benefit from salting a day ahead, while smaller cuts and fish can be seasoned for a shorter length of time. I often give instructions to season throughout the cooking process as new ingredients are added to a dish. This step is important for building flavors. South Italy's cuisine doesn't shy away from salinity and finds it in various forms—salt itself, anchovies, capers, cheese—but of course feel free to adjust to your taste.

Cooking Pasta

Most of the pasta dishes here yield four to six servings per pound of pasta. Traditionally, Italians eat in courses: first *antipasto*, then *primo*, followed by *secondo*. If you plan to do the same, the pasta course should yield six servings. If you are treating the pasta as your main dish, the recipe will serve four.

Cook pasta to the recommended doneness. Al dente means the pasta still has some firmness and bite to it. Taste the pasta as it cooks, and cook until it is still firm and most of the white part in the middle has disappeared. The *'O Scarpariello* (page 106) calls for "very al dente" pasta. In this case, the pasta should still be partially raw, as it will finish cooking in the sauce with some pasta water added.

Baking

Follow the process photographs throughout the baking section to learn the basic mixing and kneading methods, and make small changes in your cooking as necessary to accommodate any differences in flour—all flours behave slightly differently depending on their freshness, fineness, and even the environment they are in. Understanding how each type of flour behaves requires experience, so while each recipe is written and tested to ensure success, the outcome will improve through repetition. (See page 203 for more information about types of flour.)

Higher temperatures cause bread to rise faster at the cost of taste, while lower temperatures contribute to a slower rise and more complex flavors—that's why I suggest cold fermenting many doughs in the refrigerator before baking. When I say "room temperature," I always mean 71°F to 77°F. With a bit of tweaking to adapt to your environment, you should be able to reproduce these doughs just about anywhere.

THE SOUTH
ITALY KITCHEN

Equipment

Visiting a home kitchen in the south is often a trip through history, as copper pots, vintage pasta-making tools, and other heirlooms mingle with contemporary items. You don't need two-hundred-year-old implements to cook the recipes here—though if you have some, know that I am extremely jealous.

The arsenal of tools is basic and practical, much like the cuisine itself, so you'll be able to cook in the style of the south no matter where you are. A handful of recipes call for special equipment—a *ferretto* (see page 86), a thin metal rod, for forming *filjie* and *carrati* (see page 92), for example—but most can be adapted; wherever possible, I have provided alternatives for special equipment. But here are a few things you *do* need.

Pots, Pans, and Skillets

Use pots, pans, and skillets made with thicker materials to ensure consistent cooking temperatures and to avoid "hot spots" where food sticks and scorches. You'll need a cast iron pan or 100 percent metal pan without any nonstick coating for making *Focaccia Pugliese* (page 178) to create the "fried" effect on the bottom of the dough.

Finish pasta dishes in their sauces in a pan at least 2 to 3 inches deep. You'll need the extra height to facilitate tossing and swirling the pasta as it cooks. A heavy sauté pan with medium-high straight sides about 8 inches deep and a tight-fitting lid works best for braising meats. Choose a pan size that allows the ingredients to fit snugly and cook closely together.

Containers

You'll need small or medium glass jars for storing *Verdure Sott'Olio* (page 51) and nonreactive containers for soaking beans and legumes for many of the soup recipes. Use a glass container with a cover for *Olive Salate* (page 50). Large jars will come in handy for *Limoncello* (page 233), *Nucillo* (page 244), Rich Simple Syrup (page 241), and almost every recipe in the *Liquori e Cocktail* chapter.

Baking

Baking dishes and pans come in various shapes, sizes, and materials. If you don't have the size recommended in the recipe, you can certainly use a smaller or larger vessel, but be aware that doing so may affect cooking time, so adjust accordingly.

For making bread, pizza, and pastries, weighing ingredients is a crucial step to success. Cup measures can vary significantly, and different flours have slightly differing weights per cup, so using a digital scale with metric units is the only foolproof method for ensuring you achieve the intended results.

You'll need small, medium, and large bowls, preferably glass, stainless steel, or plastic, for mixing doughs, *Lievito Madre* (page 205), *Friselle Biga* (page 197) and *Pigna Biga* (page 217).

For the best results with pizza and bread, I highly recommend investing in a pizza stone. Inverted baking sheets make a good substitute. In either case, preheat the stone or baking sheet in the oven for at least 45 minutes before you bake. If you don't have a pizza peel you can improvise one with a flat, thin wooden board or a rimless baking sheet. I give detailed instructions for how to do so in the Note on page 192.

A dough scraper (also known as a bench scraper) is useful when handling and transferring dough. It also works wonders for cleaning your work surface and for dividing dough into segments. You can also use it for incising a loaf before baking it, as for *Pane di Matera* (page 198). It's also a handy tool for scraping up flour from your work surface after making fresh pasta.

Baking sheets come in different sizes, the most versatile being a half sheet (13 × 18 inches). These recipes were developed and tested using half-sheet pans, but any size should work. Always line baking sheets with parchment paper or a nonstick silicone baking mat to prevent sticking.

Pasta-Making Tools

You'll need a broad work surface, ideally wood, for making and shaping fresh pasta. Most of the pasta in this book is shaped by hand, but *filjie* and *carrati* (see page 92) use a *ferretto*, a thin rod. If you don't have one, you can improvise with a metal skewer or even a knitting needle.

Frying

In the south, most home cooks use a deep skillet, cast-iron pan, or Dutch oven instead of a deep fryer. I recommend using a pot at least 6 inches deep to help reduce the risk of spillage and splashing. Heavier materials guarantee more stable temperatures, and therefore more consistent results. Manage oil temperatures with a sturdy thermometer that can measure at least up to 400°F. It should clip to the side of the pan without touching the bottom. Use long tongs, a spider, or a metal frying basket to keep your distance from the hot oil.

Mixers

Most stand mixers come with whisk, paddle, and dough hook attachments. The latter is a great tool for kneading less hydrated and tougher dough and for long-duration mixing. I suggest using a mixer with a dough hook or paddle for making all the doughs in the *Pane, Focaccia, e Pizza* chapter. If you don't have a stand mixer, I have provided instructions for mixing by hand (page 187). Several dessert recipes require a handheld mixer.

Graters

Use a grater with very small "punched" (protruding) holes for grating Pecorino Romano, Parmigiano-Reggiano, and other hard cheeses to achieve a fine and powdery grate. Cheese grated to that consistency melts faster and more evenly and is less likely to clump. A coarser grate is best for *ricotta salata* in *Candele con 'Nduja* (page 111).

Cocktail Tools

Use a jigger or small graduated liquid measures for measuring spirits. There are a few well-stocked online outlets for cocktail tools in a range of prices listed in the resources section (page 248).

The recipes suggest specific glassware for each drink, but if you don't have it, you don't have to run out and buy it. You can use shot glasses or short tumblers for serving any of the *digestivi*.

Ingredients

Use the best-quality ingredients you can afford. Many of the recipes are incredibly simple, making inferior products very conspicuous. Look for produce and protein at their peak of freshness and flavor. Farmers' markets and community supported agriculture (CSA) organizations are good places to start. Choosing your ingredients based on freshness, seasonality, and market availability is a way to personalize the recipes in this book; this approach to shopping perfectly mirrors the cuisine of the south.

There are some items that will be an essential part of your south-style repertoire. Many are staples that are easy to track down whether you live in Naples, Italy, or Naples, Florida, while others don't yet have wide distribution in the States. I have included some online resources for specialty items on page 248.

Anchovies

In spite of the south's expansive coastline, its people have historically relied on salt- or oil-cured fish, since it is less perishable than its fresh counterpart. When choosing anchovies, I recommend the salt-packed variety over those packed in oil. Their flavor

and subtlety are far superior. Salted anchovies are available at Italian specialty stores, and there are instructions for cleaning them on page 134; you can find the oil-packed kind at supermarkets, but choose your source carefully to avoid being stuck with fish packed in rancid oil.

Black Pepper

Once an exotic spice available to only the wealthiest, black pepper is now cheap and ubiquitous. It's included in nearly every savory recipe. When a recipe calls for black pepper, use whole peppercorns and coarsely grind them fresh for each use.

Bread Crumbs

Bread crumbs are a staple in kitchens of the south and are typically made from stale good-quality bread. I call for a number of different types of bread crumbs, all of which can easily be made at home and are engineered to have much more flavor than any store-bought variety.

Eggs

Unless otherwise stated, my recipes call for large eggs. I recommend using farm-fresh organic eggs whenever possible.

Fennel Pollen

Fennel pollen beautifully complements the taste of pork and enhances the flavors in *Capocollo ai Funghi* (page 143). It is available at specialty shops and via mail order (see Resources, page 248). You can substitute finely ground dried fennel seeds (grind them as you need them).

Flour

Use organic *farina di semola* (durum wheat flour) for making fresh pastas like orecchiette (see page 90) and *raschiatelli* (see page 90).

The bread and pizza recipes call for bread flour and all-purpose flour, both of which are widely available in supermarkets. *Pane di Matera* uses *farina di semola rimacinata* (fancy durum flour), which is sold in specialty shops and online. There is naturally some variation between bags of flour, even those of the same brand, which means flours will absorb water at different rates. For best results, use the freshest flour you can find. For a deep dive into what makes these flours different from one another and adapted to either pizza or bread, read the feature on page 203.

Lard

Use good-quality lard from ethically raised pigs.

Oil

Unless otherwise noted, always use extra-virgin olive oil (see page 49), whether for rending pancetta fat, cooking vegetables, or dressing a salad. For frying, use any neutral oil with a high smoke point, such as grapeseed, canola, peanut, or corn.

Pasta

For the dried pasta recipes, use only high-quality slow-dried bronze-extruded durum wheat pasta. It has excellent structure and flavor, and is a key ingredient in a dish. High-end brands like Pastificio dei Campi, Benedetto Cavalieri, Mancini, Pastificio Felicetti, and Setaro are worth the $8 to $10 splurge.

In each dish, I specify a pasta shape and give suggestions on how to mix and match condiments. The dried pasta arsenal of the south includes spaghetti, ziti, and *paccheri*.

Peperoncino

The southern palate isn't afraid of a little heat and employs *peperoncino*, a mild to moderate-strength chile, as a staple. I use a lot of dried *peperoncino* here—market stalls sell it from hanging strands—but you can use red pepper flakes for mild heat or fresh Thai bird's eye chile for a more piquant effect.

Salt

Always use sea salt, unless otherwise noted.

Tomatoes

Use canned whole tomatoes rather than crushed. The latter tend to be made with scraps and are therefore of inferior quality. Many canned tomato brands imply that their Italian origins are shorthand for quality, but not all Italian brands use quality tomatoes. When purchasing tomatoes declaring "Made in Italy" on the label, it pays to be skeptical of what's in the can or jar. The resources section (page 248) lists suggested retailers for tracking down great-quality Italian products via mail order. Don't overlook American brands like Bianco DiNapoli, which are organic and hand-selected to ensure maximum quality.

Vinegar

Use only good-quality vinegar for recipes like *Scapece alla Gallipolina* (page 127). Poor-quality vinegars lack subtly and balance, and will ruin your dish.

I will reference these pages throughout the book so you can look at them as needed. With the basics I've laid out here and what you already have at home, you're ready to reproduce these recipes, no matter how close or far from the Italian south you are!

ANTIPASTI

—

STARTERS

MANELL'

Fried Polenta Fritters

Serves 4 to 6

2⅔ cups instant polenta

⅓ cup small-diced *cicioli* (see Note)

2 tablespoons extra-virgin olive oil

Sea salt and freshly ground black
pepper

1 cup boiling water

Neutral oil (see page 37) or lard,
for frying

At Trattoria Masella, a working farm in Cerreto
Sannita (near Benevento) with a restaurant and rooms
for rent, a snarling dog defends the pigsty. On one
recent trip to this family-run establishment, proprietor
Dino held his protective canine back as I inspected his
hogs, a couple dozen happy animals who supply the
farm and restaurant with meat and fat. The area around
the farm, which sits at the edge of steep Apennine
peaks, is known for rustic mountain fare that never
wastes. Even the scraps left over from rendering
pork fat are used, making their way into dishes as
a savory flavoring known as *cicioli*. For *manell'*, so
called because they take the form of one's hand (*mano*)
as they are shaped, *cicioli* are mixed with cornmeal.
These fritters are served at festive meals and especially
holidays, but Dino or his mother, Maria, will make
them upon request at their trattoria.

Line a large platter or baking sheet with paper towels.

In a medium bowl, mix together the instant polenta,
cicioli, olive oil, salt, and pepper. Add the boiling water,
about ¼ cup at a time, mixing vigorously to incorporate
all the ingredients until a compact mass has formed.

In a medium frying pan or cast-iron skillet, heat 2 inches
of oil to 400°F.

When the corn mixture is cool enough to handle, grab
a fistful and squeeze it between your palm and fingers,
creating a crescent-shaped fritter with your fist.
Repeat. Fry the *manell'*, working in batches as needed,
turning once for even browning, about 4 minutes. Drain
on the lined platter and serve hot, sprinkled with salt.

NOTE Cicioli are a common ingredient in the south, but
they come in various incarnations depending on where you
are. Sometimes they are pressed fat, layered, and sliced to be
used like fatback or pancetta. In this case, they are the fatty
and meaty substance that has been left behind when pig fat
is rendered. The remaining material is pressed into tiles and
used to impart savory flavor. If you cannot find *cicioli*, you
can substitute pancetta, *guanciale*, or *lardo*.

Mozzarella di Bufala
Buffalo Mozzarella

Time is the enemy of *mozzarella di bufala*, mozzarella made from the milk of water buffalo. When this fresh cheese turns two days old, it begins to lose its juiciness, and its sweet lactic flavors turn to biting acidity. The most fastidious mozzarella consumers won't even eat day-old stuff. At Tenuta Vannulo in Capaccio, that's not even an option. The farm's five hundred water buffalo produce milk for mozzarella that sells out every day by early afternoon. It's the only place in the world to get the farm's cheese.

Vannulo is set just off the SS18, an unsightly stretch of state road that connects the A2 highway to the hulking, honey-hued Greek temples at Paestum. Tonino Palmieri has been making cheese on his family's farm there since 1988. Vannulo operates a café serving yogurt and gelato, a restaurant, and, most important, a shop where they sell their small-batch mozzarella. To ensure the best-quality product, they don't have any off-site distribution.

Tonino's grandfather began raising water buffalo for their milk about a century earlier, but Tonino was the first in his family to enter the production arena. His devotion to quality has enabled him to create a completely closed system. The mozzarella is made exclusively by hand and only with the milk from the farm. It is combined with whey "starter" from the previous day's production and veal rennet. The resulting curd is broken twice, then left to ferment under the whey for 3 to 4 hours. Next, the *filatura* (stretching process) forces water from the cheese before the final step, shaping. The cheese is *mozzato* (pinched) into shapes: *bocconcini* (tiny balls), *trecce* (braids), *palle* (balls), and *nodi* (knots).

The global demand for *mozzarella di bufala* means Italy's water buffalo are exploited to produce as much milk as possible, naturally to the detriment of their well-being. Indeed, most farms sell their milk to large, industrial producers. Not Tonino, though. In contrast, the water buffalo at Vannulo are the happiest animals you'll find anywhere in the region. Their stalls are mechanized to allow them to take cool showers at will. They autoregulate their own spa treatments—their weight triggers moving bristles that clean and massage their rough black skin. They only eat food produced on Tenuta Vannulo's 110 hectares, each consuming around 50 pounds of fresh herbs daily. When they want to rest, they retreat to rubber mattresses. It's hard to imagine that any water buffalo have ever had it so good since they landed in Italy in the Middle Ages—and I swear you can taste the difference in their milk.

PEPERONI IMBOTTITI ALLA BENEVENTANA

Bread-Stuffed Peppers

Serves 4 to 6

2 cups soft bread crumbs

1 ripe tomato, chopped

¼ cup black olives, rinsed, pitted, and chopped

4 anchovy fillets, cleaned (see page 134) and chopped

1 tablespoon capers, rinsed and chopped

1 egg, beaten

¼ cup plus 2 tablespoons extra-virgin olive oil

1 teaspoon dried oregano

1 garlic clove, finely chopped

¼ cup finely grated Parmigiano-Reggiano

Sea salt

2 pounds red peppers (ideally long or short horn-shaped red peppers), tops and seeds removed

Dozens of pepper varieties thrive in the soil of Campania. The flat and bulbous *papaccella* is pickled and served with pork; bell peppers are halved, sprinkled with bread crumbs, and baked until caramelized and nearly falling apart; and the horn-shaped *cornetto* is stuffed with seasoned bread crumbs and gently cooked in oil. The filling changes from village to village—and even from house to house—but in Benevento, an ancient city deep in Campania, you may find olives, anchovies, capers, pine nuts, or even raisins in the bread crumb mixture. Some also add canned tuna, while others prefer Parmigiano-Reggiano, but all cook the peppers until they nearly burst open, spilling out their flavorful contents.

In a large bowl, mix together the bread crumbs, tomato, olives, anchovies, capers, egg, ¼ cup of the olive oil, oregano, garlic, and Parmigiano-Reggiano. Season with salt, taking care not to add too much, as the capers and olives are already salty. Stuff the peppers loosely to the tops with the bread mixture.

In a large skillet, heat the remaining 2 tablespoons olive oil over medium heat. When the oil begins to shimmer, add the stuffed peppers and cook, turning occasionally, until the peppers are cooked through and very soft, about 20 minutes for small ones, 25 minutes for larger ones. Serve immediately or at room temperature.

FRITTELLE DI ZUCCHINE

Zucchini Patties

Makes about 15 patties,
to serve 4 to 6

---

3 cups grated zucchini (about
   2 medium zucchini)

½ cup fresh mint or parsley, chopped

3 eggs, beaten

½ cup finely grated Pecorino Romano

Sea salt

¾ cup all-purpose flour

½ cup extra-virgin olive oil,
   for frying

Summer in the south is a season of grilled zucchini, fried zucchini, fried and marinated zucchini, stuffed zucchini, baked zucchini . . . This New World import is abundant in the summer months, so cooks have invented all sorts of ways to use it up. These zucchini patties offer a super-simple way to do just that. If you have zucchini flowers, you can tear them and fold them into the batter, too.

Line a large platter or baking sheet with paper towels.

In a medium bowl, mix together the zucchini, mint, eggs, Pecorino Romano, and a generous pinch of salt. Add the flour and mix well, eliminating any lumps. The batter should be thick and pourable.

In a large frying pan or cast-iron skillet, heat the olive oil over medium heat. When the oil begins to shimmer, working in batches, spoon the zucchini mixture into the pan with a large spoon, making discs between ¼ and ½ inch thick and roughly 3 inches in diameter. Fry the fritters until you see even browning coming up the sides, about 2 minutes, then flip and fry until browned on the second side, about 2 minutes more. To prevent hot oil splatters, steer the oil to the bottom of the pan and flip the fritter toward the top of the pan.

Drain the fritters on the lined platter, sprinkle with salt, and serve immediately or at room temperature.

NOTE Zucchini, like all produce, develops throughout its growing season. It is sweet early in the season and may develop bitterness later on. To see where your zucchini is in the seasonal spectrum, just take a bite. If the zucchini is very bitter, salt it in advance. Place the grated zucchini in a colander set over a bowl or the sink and sprinkle it with salt. Allow the zucchini to sit for an hour or so; some liquid will drain out. Squeeze out the excess liquid before transferring to a bowl to combine.

Olio Extravirgine di Oliva
Extra-Virgin Olive Oil

Like grapes, olives were domesticated in Asia Minor—and slowly migrated west into the Mediterranean basin. By the eighth century BC, olives and their oil were an important commercial product in Italy's Phoenician and Greek colonies; their role as an ingredient for cooking, cosmetics, and fuel only intensified during Roman times, when any area with a climate amenable to olive production participated in the empire's robust global oil trade.

Since ancient times, people on the Italian peninsula have harvested olives in the fall, pressed them into a paste, then used mills to extract the oil from the olive pulp and water. The basic methods haven't changed much over the millennia, although the pressing process has been mechanized. Most of Italy's olives—at least those destined to become extra-virgin olive oil—are still harvested by hand and pressed the same day, as they have been for thousands of years. Naturally, quality hand-harvested olives come at a cost. Prices for extra-virgin olive oil from Italy are much higher than prices for Spanish or Greek oils, but the quality difference is undeniable. And it's quantifiable. Olives pressed within hours of picking haven't deteriorated or developed acidity levels that create unbalanced flavor or a foul taste.

Today, olive oil is a major commercial product in the south, where conditions permit trees to grow at altitudes of up to 800 meters above sea level (as opposed to just 450 meters in northern regions). Thanks to mild climates and vast production zones, Puglia and Calabria are Italy's top oil-producing regions, contributing much of the three gallons a year that Italians consume per capita and the thirty thousand tons the country exports.

Drive through either area, and you'll see the twisted trunks of *ulivi secolari*, centuries-old olive trees. In the spring, white flowers bloom on the trees' ancient branches, which then bear fruits that are tiny at first and then grow and mature into full-fledged olives by October. There are hundreds of varieties of olive trees in Italy, but several have suffered a serious decline in the past five years. A blight called *Xylella fastidiosa* has been spreading through Salento, the heel of the Italian boot. The EU, once dedicated to protecting Puglia's olive trees, is now powerless in doing so as this bacterial disease ravages the *ulivi secolari*, moving closer to Brindisi and Bari with each harvest. You can support Puglia's oil industry by purchasing oils from the blight-adjacent areas around Brindisi, Otranto, and Bari (see Resources, page 248).

OLIVE SALATE

Cured Olives

Makes about 1 pound

1 pound raw uncured fresh olives
1 cup kosher salt

The first time I saw an olive tree in the flesh was on a school trip through Italy when I was sixteen. On my second trip, years later, I got close enough to a tree to taste its fruit (I have a habit of eating things I see growing in nature). To my surprise, it was completely inedible. Thanks to an astringent compound called oleuropein, almost all olives must be cured before they are eaten. There are numerous ways to do this. Companies processing olives in industrial quantities use lye (scary), while small producers and farmers use salt, brine, or even water. If you're lucky enough to have access to freshly harvested olives, here's how to make them taste delicious.

Place the olives and salt in a glass container that fits them snugly. Seal and set aside in a dark, cool place until the olives have lost their bitter, astringent flavor, about 6 weeks. Start tasting them after the fourth week to check their progress. The olives will keep in a sealed container in the refrigerator for several weeks, or longer if covered with extra-virgin olive oil.

VERDURE
SOTT'OLIO

Marinated Vegetables

Serves 8 to 10

FOR WILD ASPARAGUS, BROCCOLI RABE, CARROTS, ARTICHOKE HEARTS, ONIONS, OR MUSHROOMS

3 cups good-quality white wine vinegar, plus more as needed

3 cups water

3 tablespoons sea salt, plus more as needed

3 tablespoons sugar, plus more as needed

3 bay leaves

1 teaspoon whole black peppercorns

1 pound wild asparagus, broccoli rabe, carrots (cut into ¼-inch-thick slices), artichoke hearts (halved), onions (halved and cut into ¼-inch-thick slices), or mushrooms (halved)

Leaves from 10 sprigs fresh thyme

Extra-virgin olive oil

FOR RED OR YELLOW BELL PEPPERS

1 pound red or yellow bell peppers

Sea salt

1 tablespoon salted capers, rinsed

2 garlic cloves, thinly sliced

Extra-virgin olive oil

FOR EGGPLANTS

2 medium eggplants, cut into ¼-inch-thick rounds

Sea salt

¼ cup fresh mint leaves

Extra-virgin olive oil

Until just a few decades ago, virtually every country kitchen in the south would have been equipped with tools for harvesting and drying fruits and vegetables so they could be preserved for future use. Nothing was ever wasted, and there was an intense necessity to preserve abundant summer produce for the impending winter. Today, implements like hay mats used to dry figs and tomatoes have either been chucked out or relegated to wall hangings as decorative reminders of a rural past. On rare occasions, while driving through the olive groves around Lecce, you might spy some halved tomatoes or peppers laid out to dry naturally in the sun on the roofs of stone buildings called *pagghiare*, while you're more likely to find eggplants strung up to dry in the remote villages of Parco del Pollino in Basilicata. Homemade preserved produce is less common than it once was, but I would wager there isn't a single kitchen in the south that doesn't at least have a jar of sun-dried tomatoes.

Serve the *verdure sott'olio* with cheese, on *bruschette*, or on their own as part of a larger *antipasto* spread.

In a medium pot, bring the vinegar and water to a simmer over low heat. Add the salt and sugar. When both have dissolved, taste the brine; it should taste balanced, like something you would use to dress salad. Adjust as needed, then add the bay leaves, peppercorns, and asparagus, broccoli rabe, carrots, artichoke hearts, onions, or mushrooms. Cook each vegetable individually, working in batches, until they are al dente. Drain, set aside to cool completely, and pat dry with paper towels. Layer the cooled vegetables and thyme into glass jars and add olive oil to cover. Seal the jars and store in the refrigerator for up to 1 week.

Grill the bell peppers on a hot grill or in a grill pan, turning as needed, until the skin is charred all over, about 10 minutes. Transfer to a brown paper bag or airtight plastic container, seal, and let cool completely, about 30 minutes. Peel off and discard the charred skin. Cut the peppers into ½-inch strips, scraping off and discarding the seeds. Season with salt to taste. Layer the cooled peppers, capers, and garlic in glass jars and add olive oil to cover. Seal the jars and store in the refrigerator for up to 1 week.

Grill the eggplant rounds on a hot grill or in a grill pan, turning as needed, until evenly charred, about 5 minutes. Set aside to cool, about 10 minutes. Season with salt to taste. Layer the cooled eggplants and mint

(recipe continues)

FOR ROASTED TOMATOES

1 pound small cherry tomatoes, halved

Large pinch of sea salt, plus more
   as needed

1 teaspoon dried oregano

Extra-virgin olive oil

FOR STUFFED CHERRY PEPPERS

3 cups good-quality white wine
   vinegar, plus more as needed

3 cups water

3 tablespoons sea salt, plus more as
   needed

3 tablespoons sugar, plus more as
   needed

1 pound cherry peppers, tops and
   seeds removed

1 tablespoon salted capers, rinsed and
   chopped

2 (5-ounce) cans tuna in oil

2 salted anchovy fillets, cleaned (see
   page 134) and cut into ½-inch pieces

Extra-virgin olive oil

in glass jars and add olive oil to cover. Seal the jars and
store in the refrigerator for up to 1 week.

Preheat the oven to 225°F. Line a baking sheet with
parchment paper.

Place the tomatoes cut-side up on the prepared baking
sheet. Sprinkle with the salt and oregano. Bake for
2 to 2½ hours, until the tomatoes shrivel and shrink
by about half. Remove from the oven and allow to cool
completely. Season with salt to taste. Layer the cooled
tomatoes and oregano in glass jars and add olive oil to
cover. Seal the jars and store in the refrigerator for up
to 1 week.

In a medium pot, bring the vinegar and water to a
simmer over low heat. Add the salt and sugar. When
both have dissolved, taste the brine; it should taste
balanced, like something you would use to dress a salad.
Adjust as needed, then add the cherry peppers and
cook until al dente, about 4 minutes. Drain, set aside to
cool completely, and pat dry with paper towels. Season
with salt to taste.

Meanwhile, in a medium bowl, combine the capers, tuna,
and anchovies. Mash with a fork until the mixture has
nearly formed a paste.

Fill the cooled cherry peppers with the tuna mixture.
Place the stuffed peppers in glass jars and add olive oil
to cover. Seal the jars and store in the refrigerator for
up to 1 week.

FRITTATA AI FIORI

Frittata with Spring
Flowers

*Serves 4 to 6 as a starter
or 2 to 4 as a main*

8 eggs

Sea salt and freshly ground black
  pepper

1 cup *fiori di sambuco* (elderflower
  blossoms), plus more for garnish

¼ cup extra-virgin olive oil

In May, the hills around Cosenza in northern Calabria are blanketed in patches of yellow and white. The yellow hue is from *ginestra*, a flowering plant ubiquitous just about everywhere south of Naples with fibrous stalks once used for clothing. The white patches are *fiori di sambuco*, elderflower blossoms (no relation to the clear, anise-and-fennel-flavored Sambuca liqueur popular in central Italy), which are harvested and folded into *frittate* to impart a slightly sweet and floral flavor. You may have *fiori di sambuco* in your own backyard—it grows across North America—but if not, you can substitute borage, acacia, nasturtium, or other edible flowers. If using zucchini flowers, remove the pistils and clean the flowers gently before using.

Preheat the oven to 375°F.

In a large bowl, whisk the eggs with salt and pepper to taste. Gently stir in the flowers.

Heat the olive oil in a large ovenproof skillet over low heat. When the oil begins to shimmer, add the egg mixture. Using a wooden spoon, stir a few times, moving from the outside of the pan toward the center. When the eggs begin to set around the edges, turn off the heat and transfer the pan to the oven. Bake the frittata for 10 to 15 minutes, until the edges start to come away from the sides of the pan and the center starts to rise.

Remove the pan from the oven and allow the frittata to cool before unmolding, about 30 minutes. To unmold, run a heatproof spatula around the edges and underneath the frittata and slide it onto a serving plate. Serve at room temperature, sliced into wedges and garnished with additional flowers.

POLPETTE CASCE E OVO

Bread "Meatballs"

Serves 4 to 6 as a starter

---

4 cups cubed stale bread with crusts

5 eggs, beaten

¾ cup finely grated Pecorino Romano

Sea salt and freshly ground black pepper

2 tablespoons extra-virgin olive oil

1 onion, diced

1 (14-ounce) can whole tomatoes, crushed by hand

4 or 5 fresh basil leaves, torn

South Italy's menus are full of balls—meatballs, fish balls, and even bread balls. Frugal cooks who needed to use every last food scrap created all sorts of recipes to make the most of their stale bread. And in many villages, bread would be baked in communal ovens just once a week, so stale bread– and bread crumb– based recipes were particularly prevalent. Today, the custom of using every crumb has vanished—bakeries and supermarkets sell bread super cheap and daily— but bread balls are still very popular in the south. To serve this dish as a main course for four to six, double the recipe.

In a large bowl, combine the bread, eggs, Pecorino Romano, salt, and pepper. Mix thoroughly by hand.

Heat the olive oil in a large saucepan over medium-low heat. When the oil begins to shimmer, add the onion. Season with salt and cook, stirring, until soft and translucent, about 15 minutes. Add the tomatoes, season with salt, and cook until the sauce thickens and the tomatoes have lost their raw flavor, about 10 minutes more. Stir in the basil leaves.

While the sauce is cooking, using your hands, form the bread mixture into balls roughly the size of walnuts.

Transfer the balls to the pan with the tomato sauce, increase the heat to medium, and cook, undisturbed, for about 5 minutes to allow the balls set up. Cook, turning occasionally, until the balls are cooked through and slightly firm to the touch, about 15 minutes more. If the sauce gets too thick, add water to the pan as needed, pouring it in at the sides of the pan. Serve warm or at room temperature.

NOTE If the bread mixture is sticky, wet your hands with warm water before rolling it into balls.

MELANZANE A' SCARPONE

Stuffed Eggplants

Serves 6

¼ cup extra-virgin olive oil, plus more
for greasing

6 small eggplants, halved lengthwise

Sea salt

2 onions, diced

¼ cup Gaeta olives, rinsed, drained,
pitted, and roughly chopped

1 tablespoon capers, rinsed, drained,
and roughly chopped

¼ cup tomato sauce

8 ounces mozzarella or *scamorza*
cheese, cut into ½-inch cubes

¼ cup water

The city of Naples is packed with simple trattorias, like Cibi Cotti in the Mergellina Market and Osteria Donna Teresa in Vomero, where items are priced between 3 and 5 euros to attract budget-conscious locals. Many dishes are baked just before service (often in wonderfully seasoned cast-iron pans) and served at room temperature throughout the day. More than a few of these staples feature stuffed vegetables; *melanzane a' scarpone*, eggplant cooked until it nearly falls apart, is among them. In Naples, you will encounter a much oilier version than what I've shared here. If you wish to authentically replicate, simply double the listed olive oil quantity.

Eggplants, like tomatoes, peppers, and tobacco, are part of the nightshade family, a group of plants containing alkaloids that cause bitterness. Cooking eggplants (and in the south, we always do) breaks down that compound, eliminating bitterness, so there's no need to salt them in advance.

Preheat the oven to 350°F. Grease a baking dish large enough to fit the eggplant halves snugly.

Place the eggplants in the prepared baking dish, skin-side down. Season with salt and bake until soft and creamy, 25 to 40 minutes. Remove from the oven, leaving the oven on. Allow the eggplants to cool slightly, then scoop the flesh into a large bowl using a knife or melon baller, leaving about ¼ inch of flesh on the skin. Return the eggplant shells to the baking dish, skin-side down.

Heat the olive oil in a large saucepan over medium-low heat. When the oil begins to shimmer, add the onions. Season with salt and cook, stirring, until the onions become soft and translucent, about 15 minutes. Add the olives and capers and bloom in the hot oil for about a minute, then add the tomato sauce, season with salt, and cook until the sauce reduces slightly, a few minutes more. Add the eggplant flesh, stir, and cook for about 5 minutes to allow the flavors to marry.

Using a spoon, divide the mixture between the eggplant shells. Scatter the mozzarella evenly over the filling. Add the water to the bottom of the baking dish, cover the dish with aluminum foil, and bake until the eggplant shells begin to lose their shape, about 25 minutes. Serve warm or at room temperature.

CAPUNATA CON *FRISELLE*

Endive, Tomato, Tuna,
and Mozzarella
with Twice-Baked
Pugliese Bread

Serves 4 to 6

1 garlic clove

4 *Friselle* (page 196)

3 tablespoons water

2 cups packed curly endive, chopped

8 salted anchovy fillets, cleaned (see page 134) and cut into ½-inch pieces

¼ cup Gaeta olives, rinsed, pitted, and chopped

1 cup cherry tomatoes, halved

2 celery ribs, cut into ½-inch pieces

1 tablespoon capers, rinsed

1 (5-ounce) can tuna in oil, drained

8 ounces *mozzarella di bufala*, cut into ¾-inch cubes

8 fresh basil leaves, torn

¼ cup extra-virgin olive oil

2 tablespoons red wine vinegar

Sea salt and freshly ground black pepper

Friselle are South Italy's answer to rusk and hardtack, dried breads that were practical, shelf-stable foods for fishermen. Fishing boats would leave Pisciotta, Scilla, Bari, and other coastal towns on long voyages in search of tuna and swordfish, and nonperishable foods like *friselle* would anchor meals during those outings. To soften these hard breads and render them edible, fishermen would sprinkle them with seawater. Today, home cooks use water from their kitchen sink instead, and you can, too. Simply drizzle a bit of water over the *friselle* and let them sit until softened, then break them up into pieces, kind of like big croutons. They pair well with summer produce, especially *capunata*, a fresh seasonal salad that should not be confused with Sicilian *caponata* (sweet-and-sour eggplant). It's the perfect combination for a no-fuss, healthy, South Italy–inspired salad or lunch on a hot day.

Rub the raw garlic over the *friselle*'s rough surface. Break the *friselle* into chunks and place in a large shallow bowl. Discard the garlic. Drizzle the water over the *friselle* and set aside to soak until softened.

In a large bowl, mix together the endive, anchovies, olives, tomatoes, celery, capers, tuna, mozzarella, basil, olive oil, and vinegar.

Drain any excess water from the bowl with the *friselle*. Add the *friselle* to the endive mixture. Toss well, season with salt and pepper, then allow the mixture to marinate for at least 15 minutes before serving.

PORCINI IMPANATI

Fried Porcini Mushrooms

Serves 4 to 6

1 cup all-purpose flour

4 eggs

4 cups bread crumbs

Sea salt

1 pound fresh porcini mushrooms, cut lengthwise into ¼-inch-thick slices

Neutral oil (see page 37), for frying

1 tablespoon roughly chopped fresh flat-leaf parsley

The woods of Calabria's Parco Nazionale della Sila are thick with larch pines and chestnut trees, their canopy of branches offering shade and trapping humidity to create the ideal conditions for porcini and other mushrooms to grow. Visit Calabria's mountainous villages in the fall to find heaps of porcini sold from the trunks of foragers parked on the side of the road.

In homes and restaurants, porcini are prepared in dozens of ways, including deep-fried. In the Sila, this starter is served on its own, unadorned except for the occasional sprinkling of parsley. If you wish to lighten things up a bit, serve a wedge of lemon on the side to provide an acidic note to cut through the fat.

Porcini mushrooms are cheap and abundant in Italy during the fall. If you don't have an affordable source in your part of the world, substitute portobello or cremini mushrooms or even king oyster mushrooms, which are widely available at Asian markets.

Line a large platter or baking sheet with paper towels.

Set up the breading station: Place the flour in a shallow medium bowl. Beat the eggs in a medium bowl. Place the bread crumbs in a shallow medium bowl. Season the flour, eggs, and bread crumbs with salt.

Dredge each mushroom slice first in flour, shaking off excess, then dip in egg, allowing excess to drip off, and finally coat in bread crumbs. Set aside.

In a medium frying pan or cast-iron skillet, heat 2 inches of oil to 350°F. Working in batches as needed, fry the breaded mushroom slices until deep golden brown, turning once to ensure even browning, 4 to 5 minutes.

Drain on the lined platter, sprinkle with salt, and serve hot, garnished with the parsley.

ZUPPE E MINESTRE

—

SOUPS AND STEWS

CRAPIATA

Fava, Pea, and
Cicerchie Soup

Serves 6 to 8

½ cup dried *farro* (emmer), soaked overnight and drained

½ cup dried wheat berries, soaked overnight and drained

½ cup dried fava beans, soaked overnight and drained

½ cup dried chickpeas, soaked overnight and drained

½ cup dried verdolini or cannellini beans, soaked overnight and drained

½ cup dried *cicerchie*, soaked overnight, blanched, and drained (see Note)

Sea salt

½ pound new potatoes, halved

2 small onions, diced

3 medium carrots, diced

3 celery stalks, diced

Freshly ground black pepper

Extra-virgin olive oil

La crapiata, or *la crapiet* as it is known in Matera's dialect, is a traditional soup made in early August to celebrate the end of the grain harvest. According to locals, the name derives from the Latin word for drunkenness, *crapula,* a fitting title considering *la crapiet* was just one ingredient for the festivities—there were also copious amounts of red wine and dancing under the moonlight. Preparation began in late July, when the women of Matera would clean grain, chickpeas, favas, and other legumes, which they would soak overnight and then cook in huge copper cauldrons over open flames in the courtyards of Matera's nativity-like rock-hewn dwellings. *Materani* used local Fagioli di Sarconi, small white verdolini beans, but you can use cannellinis. This version of the recipe is an ancient one, but other versions include tomatoes, which entered the local diet in the eighteenth century. *Crapiata* is traditionally served cold, a refreshing contrast to the hot wind that blows over Matera and the adjacent Murgia plateau in the dead of summer.

The legumes should be soaked before cooking. Place the *farro,* wheat berries, favas, chickpeas, and beans in a large container and the *cicerchie* (grass peas) in a separate large container. Add three times their volume of water and soak for 8 hours or overnight. To prepare the *cicerchie,* drain and blanch separately three times, discarding the water after each time, before using.

Place the *farro,* wheat berries, favas, chickpeas, beans, and *cicerchie* in a large pot and add enough water to cover by an inch or two. Season with salt and bring to a simmer over low heat. When the beans and grains are almost tender, or three-quarters cooked through, about 1 hour, add the potatoes, onions, carrots, and celery and season with salt. Cook until the legumes and vegetables are cooked through, about 30 minutes more. Season with more salt and pepper to taste.

Serve warm or tepid with olive oil drizzled on top.

NOTE Cicerchie (grass peas), a high-protein legume used mainly for animal feed in the United States, contains a neurotoxin that can be harmful if consumed in large quantities, as it has been in Europe following disasters and famines. To prepare *cicerchie* safely, simply blanch several times after soaking it. This ancient legume has been a staple in the south for more than two thousand years, thanks to its resistance to drought and floods. You can find it in specialty stores and online.

PIZZ E FOJE

Polenta with Wild Greens

Serves 4 to 6

FOR THE POLENTA

3 tablespoons extra-virgin olive oil, plus more for greasing

1 cup cornmeal (see Note)

½ cup all-purpose flour

1 teaspoon sea salt

1 teaspoon sugar

1 cup boiling water

1 egg, beaten

FOR THE GREENS

Sea salt

2 pounds mixed Swiss chard, dandelion greens, and wild cardoons

½ cup plus 2 tablespoons extra-virgin olive oil

2 garlic cloves, smashed

1 teaspoon *peperoncino* or red pepper flakes

NOTE To an even greater extent than flour, cornmeal ranges wildly in cup weight. A cup ranges from 120 to 200 grams, depending on the freshness and quality of the corn and how coarse or fine the grind. This recipe was tested with 200 grams coarse cornmeal.

This peasant dish from Campobasso's La Grotta di Zi' Concetta is pure comfort food. Traditionally made from wild foraged greens and stale polenta, the recipe combines bitter and herbal leafy greens with savory and sweet peasant corn bread, which are married in a pan with a healthy dose of olive oil. In Molise, the mixture of greens changes with the season and the geography. The recipe works with a wide array such as borage, wild cardoons, dandelion greens, chard, beet greens, mustard greens, broccoli rabe, or escarole, any of which you can use individually or mixed together in any proportion you wish.

Make the polenta: Preheat the oven to 400°F. Line a baking sheet with parchment paper. Grease the parchment with olive oil.

In a large bowl, combine the cornmeal, flour, salt, sugar, and olive oil. Pour the hot water over the mixture, stirring well to eliminate lumps. Set aside at room temperature to cool, about 10 minutes, then mix in the egg.

Transfer the dough to the prepared baking sheet. Using a spatula or wooden spoon, spread the dough into a ½-inch-thick slab. Bake until the dough has hardened and lightly browned, about 30 minutes.

Meanwhile, make the greens: Bring a large pot of water to a boil over high heat. Salt the water (see page 31). When the salt has dissolved, add the greens, working in batches as needed to avoid overcrowding, and cook until soft, 5 to 10 minutes, depending on the type of greens. Allow the water to return to a boil before adding the next batch. Drain the greens and spread them out on a baking sheet to cool for about 20 minutes. When the greens are cool enough to handle, gently squeeze out some of the excess water and chop into small pieces.

Heat ½ cup olive oil in a large skillet over medium heat. When the oil begins to shimmer, add the garlic and cook until it begins to turn golden, about 5 minutes. Add the *peperoncino* and cook until fragrant, about 30 seconds, then add the boiled greens and turn to coat. Season with salt. Cook, stirring frequently, for 8 to 10 minutes, until the greens have darkened and absorbed the garlic and *peperoncino* flavors.

Break the polenta into bite-size pieces and add it to the pan, stirring to combine with the greens. Serve warm or at room temperature on a large platter, family style, with the remaining 2 tablespoons olive oil drizzled on top.

Rame e Terracotta
Copper and Terra-Cotta

As recently as the 1970s, it was common practice for women in the Italian south to bring a dowry of sorts to their marriage. Depending on the village, the bride and her family might be responsible for stocking the bedroom linens or cooking implements, or both. Bringing copper cookware to the marital home signaled that a woman was both a skilled cook as well as a valuable one, her worth bound to the metal from which the pots were wrought. In addition to their symbolic value, copper implements carried the practical purpose of being essential to the south's soulful stews, braises, and broths, which require even, moderate heat to reach their fullest expression.

Copper pots were often very large, intended for one-pot meals—only in the late nineteenth century did eating in multiple courses become the standard in Italian households of the south—and would be suspended above hot coals or wood-fueled flames to simmer vegetables, legumes, and meats. Terra-cotta, kiln-baked clay, served a similar function, although unlike copper, which heats quickly, terra-cotta is slow to warm up. This makes terra-cotta ideal for long, slow cooking, essential for tough proteins. Terra-cotta vessels called *pignate* were particularly popular in Puglia, where octopus, goat, horse, or lamb might be placed inside with seasoning, the *pignate* were either covered with a clay lid or sealed with bread dough, and the meat cooked for hours.

Not surprisingly, these items were ascribed such enormous value that many women transported them in their luggage when they emigrated to America around the turn of the twentieth century.

ZUPPA DI FAGIOLI E CASTAGNE

Bean and Chestnut Soup

Serves 4 to 6

1 tablespoon extra-virgin olive oil, plus more to finish

1 ounce pancetta, diced (about ⅛ cup)

1 onion, diced

Sea salt

2 bay leaves

Leaves from 1 sprig fresh rosemary, chopped

5 ounces dried chestnuts (1 cup), soaked overnight and drained

5 ounces borlotti or eye of the goat beans (1 cup), soaked overnight and drained

2 medium potatoes, peeled and cut into ½-inch cubes

Freshly ground black pepper

Rosemary Croutons (optional; recipe follows)

Drive or hike through any of the south's many national parks in the fall and you will surely see elderly Italians foraging for chestnuts, which grow between 200 and 1,000 meters above sea level. These harvests are destined for cellars, where they will be stored for roasting or drying for soups and stews. This hearty bean and chestnut soup is a warming seasonal dish ideal for a cold winter day no matter where you are. You can find packets of dried chestnuts in Italian specialty stores in the US or online.

Heat the olive oil in a large pot over low heat. When the oil begins to shimmer, add the pancetta and cook, stirring, until the fat has rendered, about 10 minutes. Add the onion, season with salt, and cook until softened, about 15 minutes. Add the bay leaves and rosemary and cook until fragrant, about 1 minute.

Add the chestnuts, beans, potatoes, and enough water to cover. Season with salt, increase the heat to medium, and cook, stirring occasionally, until the chestnuts and beans fall apart, about 2 hours. Remove and discard the bay leaves. Season with salt and pepper.

Remove the pot from the heat and, using an immersion blender, blend until smooth. Serve immediately, topped with rosemary croutons, if desired, and drizzled with olive oil.

Rosemary Croutons
Makes 2 cups

2 cups ½-inch cubes dry rustic bread, with or without crusts

2 tablespoons extra-virgin olive oil

2 teaspoons finely chopped fresh rosemary

Sea salt

Preheat the oven to 250°F.

In a large bowl, toss the bread cubes, olive oil, rosemary, and salt. Spread out the bread pieces on a rimmed baking sheet and bake until crispy and completely dried out, 15 to 20 minutes. Let cool completely.

The bread crumbs will keep in an airtight container at room temperature for up to 3 days.

MINESTRA DI PATANE E VERZA

Potato and Cabbage Stew

Serves 8 to 10

½ cup extra-virgin olive oil, plus more
  to finish

2 garlic cloves, smashed

2 onions, roughly chopped

Sea salt

1 *peperoncino* or 1 teaspoon red
  pepper flakes

1 medium savoy cabbage, cut into
  ¼-inch pieces

3 medium Yukon Gold potatoes,
  peeled and cut into ¼-inch pieces

2 quarts vegetable broth, warmed

1 teaspoon *peperoni cruschi* powder
  or sweet paprika

When I first read the name of this winter dish on the menu of Da Peppe in Rotonda, Basilicata, I assumed it was a brothy potato and cabbage soup. *Minestre*, in my experience, were always loose soups (see *Minestra Maritata*, page 74, for example). But the food of Basilicata and its terminology never fail to surprise me—in the best ways. I ordered the dish and was served what looked like a pale green mass of mashed potatoes, *patane* in local dialect. What the dish lacked in beauty it made up for in complexity and character. The caramelized garlic notes mingled with the sweetness of the cabbage and were bound by the structure of Rotonda's celebrated high-altitude-grown potatoes. Use Yukon Golds for a perfectly delicious substitute. (But if you can, visit Da Peppe to taste the difference.)

Heat ¼ cup of the olive oil in a large pot over medium-low heat. When the oil begins to shimmer, add the garlic and onions, season with salt, and cook until the onions become soft and translucent, about 10 minutes. Add the *peperoncino* and cook until fragrant, about 30 seconds.

Increase the heat to medium and add the cabbage and potatoes. Season with salt and cook until they begin to soften but are not yet browned, about 10 minutes. Add enough broth to cover (you may not need it all) and simmer until the potatoes and cabbage are falling apart and most of the liquid has evaporated, about 30 minutes.

Remove the pot from the heat. Add the remaining ¼ cup olive oil and mash the potatoes and cabbage using a potato masher. The mixture should have the consistency of thick mashed potatoes. Serve drizzled with olive oil and sprinkled with the *peperoni cruschi*.

Minestra Maritata
Italian Wedding Soup

I was a teenager when I first heard the phrase "Italian wedding soup." Unlike some Italian Americans, I didn't grow up eating it. I took the name literally, of course. Magazines and television hosts billed the vegetable rich, meat-studded soup as a classic recipe for nuptials. Wrong. If you've ever been to an Italian wedding, you know it would be a challenge to find hot soup anywhere in the joint. "Soup" isn't even the proper translation for *minestra*, which denotes a specific category of brothy dishes.

Minestra maritata refers, instead, to "wedded broths," nuanced flavors betrothed to one another as they are blended and simmered, achieving a liquidy, meaty, vegetal polygamy. The dish originates in the Italian south, where it takes on many forms. In northern Campania's Alto Casertano, *minestra maritata* is eaten to celebrate the annual pig slaughter. In the depths of winter, pigs are butchered and their bones are boiled with any remaining scraps of the previous year's prosciutto. The broth is enriched with dandelion greens, cardoons, and escarole, each pruned and prepared separately before they head into the meaty *minestra*.

In the Irpinia zone of southern Campania, deep in the Apennine Mountains, most recipes for this winter dish also call for *'nnoglia di maiale*, a salami made from pressed, cured pork stomach and intestines.

The pork theme continues in Naples, where *minestra maritata*, praised for its restorative properties, is served for the Feast of Santo Stefano on December 26. The Neapolitan version is richer in its meat content, perhaps owing to the wealth of Naples compared with its rural neighbors. It unifies three separate broths: pork skin and other scraps, beef shank, and hen. A dozen or so foraged and cultivated greens from around the Phlegraean Fields or Mount Vesuvius are also prepared separately before joining in.

Though there are no sure traces, immigrants from Campania probably brought their varied versions of *minestra maritata* to the United States. Some considered the soup an exclusively winter dish, while others embraced both the Christmas and Easter associations. Lacking the variety of bitter herbs available in south-central Italy, the diversity of greens was scaled back and reduced primarily to escarole. The connection to the pork slaughter ritual disappeared, small chicken meatballs crept into the equation, and a new dish, with a name similar to but decidedly divorced from its origins, was born.

The *minestra maritata* recipe here pays homage to its roots but is modified in a way that is more practical for home cooks today; rather than boil each ingredient individually, the pork and vegetables are cooked separately, then married in a single simmering pot.

MINESTRA MARITATA

Wild Herb and Pork Soup

Serves 6 to 8

---

1 pound pork spareribs

¼ pound pig skin (*cotica*)

1 pound pork bones

¾ cup pancetta or *guanciale*, diced

1 pig ear (optional)

1 pig trotter (optional)

Sea salt

5 pounds mixed greens (such as chicory, escarole, cardoons, dandelion greens, wild fennel, borage)

2 medium unseasoned pork sausages

½ cup finely grated Pecorino Romano

There are literally tens of thousands of variations, each household using a proprietary recipe with its own time-honored proportions of greens. If you have to choose just a couple, escarole and dandelion greens make a good compromise to the whole mix. Don't worry about finding pig skin, ear, or trotter (foot); many butcher shops will give them away for free or at a nice discount.

Place the ribs, pig skin, bones, pancetta, pig ear (if using), and trotter (if using) in a large pot and add enough water to cover. Bring to a gentle simmer over low heat, skimming off any scum that rises to the top.

Meanwhile, bring a large pot of water to a boil over high heat. Salt the water (see page 31). When the salt has dissolved, add the greens, working in batches as needed to avoid overcrowding, and boil for 30 seconds to 1 minute. The greens should still be very al dente. Drain the greens and repeat with the remainder, allowing the water to return to a boil after each batch. Spread the greens out on a baking sheet to cool for about 20 minutes. When cool enough to handle, gently squeeze out some of the excess water and chop into 1-inch strips.

When the ribs and pig skin are tender, 2½ to 3 hours, remove the ribs, skin, bones, ear, and trotter from the broth and set aside. Add the sausages to the pot and cook on low for 10 minutes, just until cooked through. Remove and set aside. Strain the broth, then return it to the heat. Pick the meat off the ribs and trotter, reserving the meat and discarding the bones and ear. Cut the skin into a small dice. Slice the sausages into ¼-inch-thick rounds.

Add the rib meat, diced skin, any meaty bits, sausage pieces, and greens to the broth. Season with salt and simmer over low heat until the greens are very tender, about 20 minutes. Serve immediately with Pecorino dusted on top.

'A CICCIATA RI SANTA LUCIA

Bean and Grain Soup

Serves 6 to 8

½ cup extra-virgin olive oil, plus more to finish

1 large onion, diced

1 garlic clove, smashed

2 celery stalks, diced

2 medium carrots, diced

Sea salt

Pinch of *peperoncino* or red pepper flakes (optional)

¼ cup dried chickpeas, soaked overnight and drained

¼ cup dried borlotti beans, soaked overnight and drained

¼ cup dried small white beans (I like Controne), soaked overnight and drained

¼ cup dried black-eyed peas, soaked overnight and drained

¼ cup dried *farro* (emmer), soaked overnight and drained

¼ cup dried oat groats, soaked overnight and drained

¼ cup dried barley, soaked overnight and drained

¼ cup dried lentils, soaked overnight and drained

Freshly ground black pepper

¼ cup fresh parsley leaves, chopped

At the beginning of May, farmers throughout Cilento would begin planting grain and other goods. They would celebrate this time with *cicciata*, a multi-bean and grain soup dedicated to their wishes for a successful harvest. In the village of Lustra, they would combine more than a dozen beans, grains, and legumes, each soaked and simmered separately. In Centola, a similar soup was made on December 13 for the Feast of Santa Lucia with twenty types of legumes, also treated to their own individual pots. I have modified this labor-intensive process to make the recipe more practical for home cooks, which does little to diminish the hearty flavor of the soup. In a large container, soak the chickpeas, borlotti beans, white beans, and black-eyed peas in three times their volume of water for 8 hours or overnight. In a separate large container, soak the *farro*, oat groats, barley, and lentils in cold water to cover for 8 hours, overnight, or in warm water for at least 1 hour.

Heat the olive oil in a large pot over medium heat. When the oil begins to shimmer, add the onion, garlic, celery, and carrots, season with salt, and cook until softened, about 15 minutes. Add the *peperoncino* (if using) and cook until fragrant, 30 seconds more.

Add the chickpeas, borlotti beans, white beans, and black-eyed peas to the pot. Add enough water to cover by a few inches and season with salt. Reduce the heat to low and simmer until the beans are more than halfway cooked, about 45 minutes. Add the *farro*, groats, barley, and lentils and simmer until all the beans, grains, and lentils are tender, about 45 minutes more. Season with salt and black pepper. Stir in the parsley, and serve warm or tepid, with olive oil drizzled on top.

NOTE In the cuisine of South Italy, and indeed in many regional European traditions, soup, *ragù*, and braised meat recipes rely on *soffritto* (sautéed diced onion, celery, and carrots) as a base for providing flavor and depth. Every cook has her or his own preference of dice size and proportion of ingredients; some use garlic, others omit it; and old-school cooks sauté their *soffritto* in *strutto* (rendered pork fat) rather than extra-virgin olive oil.

'VUCCATA I SAN GIUSEPPE

Chickpea Soup
with Bitter Greens

Serves 4 to 6

2 cups dried chickpeas, soaked
  overnight and drained

¼ cup extra-virgin olive oil, plus more
  to finish

1 garlic clove, smashed

1 shallot, sliced

Leaves from 2 sprigs fresh rosemary,
  chopped

Sea salt

½ pound dandelion greens

Rosemary Croutons (optional;
  page 70)

While Neapolitans celebrate the Feast of San Giuseppe by devouring deep-fried cream-filled beignets, Calabrian peasants would take part in a more solemn ritual. The poor would dress up in hooded garb to cover their faces as they went door to door asking their well-to-do neighbors for food. The alms were given in the form of a protein-rich soup of chickpeas and wild greens.

Place the chickpeas in a large pot and add enough water to cover. Bring to a simmer over low heat and cook, skimming any scum that rises to the surface, for 20 to 30 minutes.

Meanwhile, heat the olive oil in a small sauté pan over medium-low heat. When the oil begins to shimmer, add the garlic, shallot, and rosemary. Season with salt and cook, stirring, until the shallot becomes soft and translucent, about 5 minutes. Remove the pot from the heat and allow the oil to cool completely—adding hot oil to water is dangerous.

Add the oil mixture to the pot with the chickpeas, season with salt, and simmer until the chickpeas are tender, about 1 hour more, adding more water as needed to keep the chickpeas covered.

Meanwhile, bring a large pot of water to a boil over high heat. Salt the water (see page 31). When the salt has dissolved, add the dandelion greens and boil for 30 seconds to 1 minute. The greens should still be very al dente. Work in batches as needed to avoid overcrowding, allowing the water to return to a boil before adding the next batch. Drain the greens and spread them out to cool on a baking sheet, about 20 minutes. When the greens are cool enough to handle, gently squeeze out some of the excess water and slice into 1-inch strips.

Add the chopped dandelion greens to the pot with the chickpeas and cook to marry the flavors, about 10 minutes more. Season with salt.

Serve the soup drizzled with olive oil and topped with croutons, if desired.

NOTE In South Italy, dandelion greens are prized for their bitter flavor. If you prefer, temper the bitterness by substituting half the dandelion greens with something milder like spinach or Swiss chard.

MINESTRA DI ZUCCHINE

Zucchini, Egg, and
Parmesan Soup

Serves 4 to 6

2 tablespoons extra-virgin olive oil

1 onion, chopped

Sea salt

2 pounds zucchini, cut into bite-size
 pieces

1 cup water

2 eggs, beaten

¾ cup finely grated Parmigiano-
 Reggiano

1 tablespoon torn fresh mint leaves

Freshly ground black pepper

In the summer months—and in mountainous areas,
well into the fall—the markets and gardens of the south
are packed with zucchini. This New World ingredient
takes many forms—round to smooth and elongated
to pale and fluted—and this seasonal soup capitalizes
on this abundance. It's essentially a summertime
stracciatella (Italian egg drop soup).

Heat the olive oil in a medium pot over medium-low heat.
When the oil begins to shimmer, add the onion. Season
with salt and cook, stirring, until the onion becomes soft
and translucent, about 15 minutes. Add the zucchini and
water, season with salt, and bring to a simmer. Cover
and simmer until the zucchini are softened and cooked
through, about 20 minutes.

Meanwhile, in a medium bowl, stir together the eggs,
Parmigiano-Reggiano, and mint.

Pour the egg mixture into the pot with the zucchini, stir,
and remove from the heat.

Season with salt and pepper and serve immediately.

LICURDIA

Tropea Onion Soup

Serves 4 to 6

---

2 tablespoons pork lard

2 pounds Tropea onions, halved and cut into ¼-inch-thick slices

Sea salt

1 tablespoon all-purpose flour

5 cups vegetable broth, warmed

6 slices rustic bread

7 ounces caciocavallo or *scamorza* cheese

Tropea onions, called torpedo onions in the US due to their elongated shape, are a variety of sweet red onions that thrive in Calabria's alluvial sand-, lime-, and clay-rich soil. They have grown in South Italy since Phoenician times, when they were both a food source and a medicinal ingredient, and today they are one of the south's most iconic indigenous species. Anywhere you look in Calabria—a trattoria, a market stall, a home kitchen—there will inevitably be a bunch of braided Tropea onions hanging on a wall. They make their way into every part of the menu (even *sorbetto* in Calabria's modern kitchens). Here they are simmered in a sweet and savory stew called *licurdia*, Calabria's answer to French onion soup.

Melt the lard in a large pot over medium-low heat. When the melted lard begins to shimmer, add the onions and season with salt. Stir, then cover and cook until the onions have wilted, 12 to 15 minutes.

Uncover, increase the heat to medium, and cook, stirring occasionally, until the onions are browned and caramelized, 25 to 30 minutes.

Dust the onions with flour and stir to combine. Slowly stir in the vegetable broth and bring to a boil. Reduce the heat to low and simmer until the onions are falling apart, about 30 minutes.

Meanwhile, preheat the broiler to high.

Place the bread slices on a baking sheet. Shave or grate the caciocavallo on top, distributing it evenly. Broil until the cheese is melted and toasty, about 2 minutes.

Serve the soup with the bruschetta on the side, or place the bruschetta, cheese-side up, atop the plated soup.

GLI
SCIUSCIELLI

Bread Dumplings with
Potato and Tomato Broth

Serves 4 to 6

2 tablespoons extra-virgin olive oil

1 onion, diced

Sea salt

1 Italian sausage link, casing removed

1 potato (I like russet), peeled and cut
into ½-inch cubes

1 (14-ounce) can tomato sauce

1 cup fresh bread crumbs

¾ cup vegetable broth, warmed

1 cup all-purpose flour

1 cup finely grated Parmigiano-
Reggiano, plus more for serving

5 eggs, beaten

⅓ cup chopped fresh flat-leaf parsley

Freshly ground black pepper

These bread dumplings come from Atena Lucana, a village of 2,300 residents in the mountainous Vallo di Diano region of southeastern Campania. In yet another example of making the most of stale bread—and another case of carbs on carbs—these bread dumplings are cooked with sliced potatoes in a brothy sauce. Potatoes add maximum caloric impact, once essential for doing hard labor in the fields.

Heat the olive oil in a large pot over medium-low heat. When the oil begins to shimmer, add the onion, season with salt, and cook until soft and translucent, about 15 minutes. Add the sausage and cook, breaking up the meat with a wooden spoon, until browned, 5 to 7 minutes, then add the potatoes. Add enough water to cover, season with salt, and bring to a boil over high heat. Reduce the heat to low and simmer for 15 minutes to marry the flavors. Add the tomato sauce, increase the heat to medium, and cook for 10 minutes more, until the potatoes are fork-tender.

Meanwhile, place the bread crumbs in a medium bowl, add the warm broth, and let soak for a few minutes, until softened. Transfer to a large bowl. Add the flour, Parmigiano-Reggiano, eggs, and parsley. Mix thoroughly by hand. The dough should form a thick, tacky paste.

Using a spoon, form the dough into egg-shaped dumplings and carefully lower them into the tomato sauce. Cook, without stirring, until the dumplings have set, about 10 minutes. Gently turn the dumplings and cook until they are cooked through and the sauce has reduced a bit, 10 minutes more. Serve immediately, dusted with some Parmigiano-Reggiano.

PASTA

—

PASTA SHAPES AND
SAUCES

Ferretto
Iron Pasta Rod

Throughout South Italy, home cooks make tubes of fresh pasta using a *ferretto*. The thin metal rod is made from iron (*ferro* in Italian); it might be custom-made or improvised with a knitting needle or bicycle spoke—I have even seen cooks use a stick or reed in a pinch.

The resulting pasta shape goes by nearly as many names as villages that produce it, but in the rural mountain village of Pietraroja, deep in Campania's Sannio region, the homemade tubes are called *carrati* (see page 92). I learned to make them from Lucia Parente, who has been crafting them her whole life. She rolls the pasta into a thick sheet and cuts it into 1-inch-long segments before pressing the *ferretto* into the dough and pushing it forward with a decisive motion to create a uniform tube, which she sets aside to rest before boiling. Lucia's technique can translate to a variety of tubular pastas, including *filjie* (see page 92), which are essentially long *carrati*.

CARRATI IN DUE MODI

Carrati Two Ways

Carrati, a hand-rolled pasta made with a *ferretto* (see page 86), is typical of Campania's Sannio region. It is served with one of two condiments, depending on the season: in the winter the pasta is paired with *ragù di castrato*, a viscous mutton sauce perfect for cold weather, while in the summer, it is tossed with ricotta and grated walnuts for a lighter, warm-weather meal. The Sannio region is known for its sheepherding, so to re-create the recipes most authentically—and flavorfully— use mutton meat and sheep's-milk ricotta. You can substitute ground beef or veal and cow's-milk ricotta, respectively, but the flavors will be much less intense.

CARRATI CON RAGÙ DI CASTRATO

Carrati with Mutton *Ragù*

Serves 4 to 6

¼ cup extra-virgin olive oil

1 pound ground mutton or veal

Sea salt

Freshly ground black pepper

2 carrots, diced

2 onions, diced

2 garlic cloves, smashed

1 bay leaf

1 cup dry white wine (I like Fiano)

1 cup *Brodo di Agnello* (lamb stock; see page 149), or water

1 pound fresh *carrati* (see page 92) or dried *cavatelli*

½ cup grated Parmigiano-Reggiano

Heat the olive oil in a large pan over medium-low heat. When the oil begins to shimmer, add the mutton, a pinch of salt and black pepper, and cook until the meat is browned and the fat is rendered, a few minutes. Move the mutton to the side of the pan and add the carrots, onions, garlic, bay leaf, and a pinch of salt and cook until the vegetables have softened, about 15 minutes. Add the wine and cook until the liquid has evaporated, about 5 minutes.

Add the stock, reduce the heat to low, and return the mixture to a simmer. Cover and cook, stirring occasionally and adding more water as needed to keep the pan from drying, for about 1½ hours.

Meanwhile, bring a large pot of water to a rolling boil over high heat. Heavily salt the water (see page 31). When the salt has dissolved, add the *carrati* and cook until the raw bite is gone, about 3 minutes. Drain the *carrati*, reserving the pasta cooking water, and add the pasta and ¼ cup of the pasta cooking water to the mutton *ragù*, stirring to coat. Add a bit more water to loosen the sauce as needed. Season with salt and pepper. Plate, sprinkle the Parmigiano-Reggiano on top, and serve immediately.

CARRATI CON RICOTTA E NOCI

Carrati with Ricotta and Walnuts

Serves 4 to 6

2 cups ricotta (I like sheep's-milk ricotta)

⅔ cup plus 3 tablespoons finely grated Parmigiano-Reggiano or Grana Padano

1½ cups roughly chopped toasted walnuts

Sea salt and freshly ground black pepper

½ pound fresh *carrati* (see page 92) or dried *cavatelli*

In a large bowl, combine the ricotta, ⅔ cup of the Parmigiano-Reggiano, 1 cup of the walnuts, and salt and pepper to taste. Mix well.

Bring a large pot of water to a rolling boil over high heat. Heavily salt the water (see page 31). When the salt has dissolved, add the *carrati* and cook until the raw bite is gone, about 3 minutes. Drain the *carrati,* reserving the pasta cooking water, and add the pasta and ¼ cup of the pasta cooking water to the ricotta mixture, stirring to coat. Add a bit more water to loosen the sauce as needed. Plate, sprinkle the remaining ½ cup walnuts and 3 tablespoons Parmigiano-Reggiano on top, and serve immediately.

ORECCHIETTE, RASCHIATELLI, E CICATIELLI

Flour-and-Water
Pasta Shapes

Makes about 1⅓ pounds

3½ cups (400 grams) *farina di semola* (semolina flour; see page 203), plus more as needed

¾ cup plus 2 tablespoons warm water

Semolina, for dusting

NOTE The raw, unshaped dough can be tightly wrapped in plastic wrap and stored in the refrigerator for up to 1 week; it does not freeze well. Shaped pasta can be tightly wrapped in plastic wrap and frozen for up to 1 week.

This basic flour-and-water dough can be used to form several pasta shapes and due to its strength and gluten potential works best with short, tight pasta shapes.

Pour the flour onto a work surface and make a fist-size well in the middle. Add the water, then mix with a fork, working from the edges of the well into the center, gradually incorporating it into the flour to form a shaggy dough. The dough should feel tacky but not sticky. If the dough sticks to your fingers, add 2 tablespoons more flour.

Knead the dough energetically until it is a smooth, compact mass, 10 to 12 minutes. Wrap the dough in plastic wrap and allow to rest at room temperature for 30 minutes before shaping.

To make all shapes, flatten the dough into a disc about ½ inch thick. Cut off a strip of dough about ½ inch wide, then follow the shaping instructions of your choice below.

To shape orecchiette: Roll the dough into a long strand about ¼ inch thick by pressing down on the dough with your fingertips in a back-and-forth motion. Press a knife into the edge of the strand and use it to drag the dough across the work surface, forming a roughly ¾-inch circular curled-up pasta shape. Set aside on a plate dusted with semolina. Repeat with the remaining dough.

To shape *raschiatelli*: Roll the dough into a long strand about ¼ inch thick by pressing down on the dough with your fingertips in a back-and-forth motion. Cut the strand into ½-inch pieces. Using your index, middle, and ring fingers, press into the far edge of each pasta piece while pressing down on the dough and rolling it toward you, dragging it along the work surface to form an irregular curled pasta shape. Set aside on a plate dusted with semolina. Repeat with the remaining dough.

To shape *cicatielli*: Roll the dough into a long strand about ¼ inch thick by pressing down on the dough with your fingertips in a back-and-forth motion. Cut the strand into 1-inch pieces. Using the end of a knife, gently press into the middle of each pasta piece while pressing down slightly and rolling it toward you to form a curled pasta tube. Set aside on a plate dusted with semolina. Repeat with the remaining dough.

Bring a large pot of water to a rolling boil over high heat. Heavily salt the water (see page 31). When the salt has dissolved, add the pasta and cook until the raw bite is gone, about 3 minutes. Serve with the condiment of your choosing.

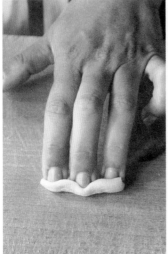

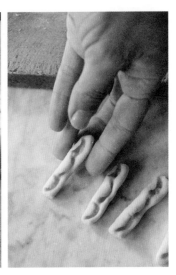

FILJIE E CARRATI

Egg Pasta Shapes

Makes about 2½ pounds

---

6 cups (1 kilogram) *farina di semola* (durum wheat flour; see page 203), plus more as needed

1 egg

2 cups plus 1 tablespoon warm water

Semolina, for dusting

This egg-enriched dough can be used to make pasta shapes like *filjie* and *carrati*, both of which are made with a metal rod called a *ferretto* (see page 86). The protein and fat from the egg give the dough a nice elasticity ideal for "wrapping" around the rod.

Pour the flour onto a work surface and make a well in the middle. Add the egg to the well and beat it with a fork. Working from the edges of the well, incorporate a bit of the flour into the egg. Add the water to the well a little at a time, gradually incorporating the flour, working from the edges into the center to form a shaggy dough. The dough should feel tacky but not sticky. If the dough sticks to your fingers, add 2 tablespoons more flour.

Knead the dough energetically until it is a smooth, compact mass, 10 to 12 minutes. Wrap the dough in plastic wrap and allow to rest at room temperature for 30 minutes, then follow the shaping instructions of your choice.

The raw, unshaped dough can be tightly wrapped in plastic wrap and stored in the refrigerator for up to 1 week; it does not freeze well. Shaped pasta can be tightly wrapped in plastic wrap and frozen for up to a week.

To shape *filjie*: Working in batches as needed, roll the dough into a rectangle about ⅛ inch thick. Cut the dough into 5 × ¼-inch pieces. Gently press a *ferretto* (see page 86) into the center of the dough and, with a decisive movement, roll the *ferretto* away from you while pressing into the dough. The dough will wrap around the *ferretto,* forming a long tube. Slide the pasta off the *ferretto* and set aside on a plate dusted with semolina. Repeat with the remaining dough.

To shape *carrati*: Working in batches as needed, roll the dough into a rectangle about ⅛ inch thick. Cut the dough into 1 × ¼-inch pieces. Gently press a *ferretto* (see page 86) at a slight diagonal into the center of the dough and, with a decisive movement, roll the *ferretto* away from you while pressing into the dough. The dough will wrap around the *ferretto,* forming a short tube. Slide the pasta off the *ferretto* and set aside on a plate dusted with semolina. Repeat with the remaining dough.

Bring a large pot of water to a rolling boil over high heat. Heavily salt the water (see page 31). When the salt has dissolved, add the pasta and cook until the raw bite is gone, about 3 minutes. Serve with the condiment of your choosing.

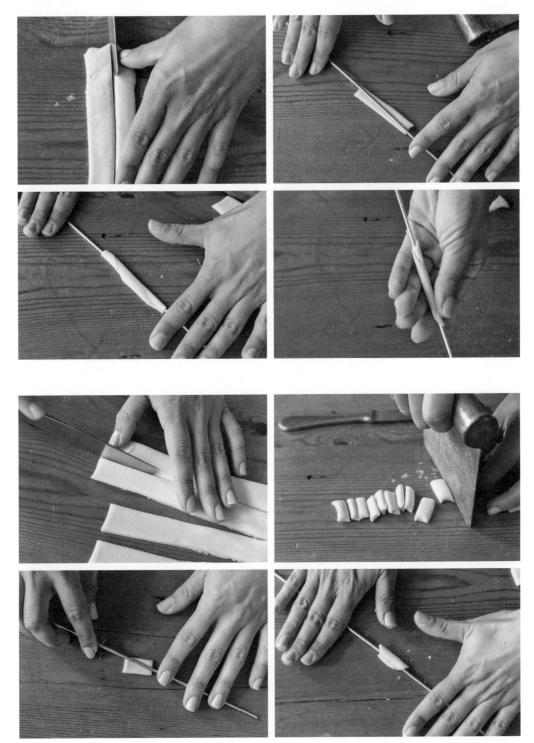

Pasta di Gragnano
Pasta from Gragnano

Giuseppe Di Martino, founder of my favorite pasta brand, Pastificio dei Campi, may like pasta more than any other human I know (and that's saying a lot). It's not *just* the family business, though the Di Martinos have been making pasta since 1912: Giuseppe is purely and unwaveringly devoted to eating pasta, which he does all over the planet. Equal parts businessman and artisan, he is just as at home on the road promoting his pasta (both his aforementioned personal brand as well as the family brand, Pastificio Di Martino) as he is in his hometown of Gragnano.

Gragnano, which overlooks the Bay of Naples, is naturally disposed to pasta production. The town center follows a crescent of terrain that traps an elliptical breeze, which delivers a constant, humid wind. Before the early twentieth century, when pasta was made by families, home cooks would hang their long spaghetti strands outside on broom handles to dry in these ideal conditions. When the pasta industry became mechanized just before the turn of the century, production moved indoors, and rather than being shaped by hand, the pasta dough began to be extruded through metal dies. The drying process was streamlined and improved, and large fans would churn air through open halls.

Today, Pastificio dei Campi dries its pasta in a way that merges technology and history. Giuseppe's pasta-drying machines are calibrated to dry the pasta slowly—24 hours for short shapes and more than 48 for long ones—in rooms that replicate Gragnano's temperature and humidity conditions gleaned from the era before climate change.

The long drying periods are essential to a quality pasta, allowing the starch and gluten to be undisturbed when they drop into the boiling water, resulting in a stronger cooked product. Consider that international companies like Barilla dry their pasta four times faster, in hot rooms, which essentially cooks the pasta before it's packaged. Giuseppe's choice of raw material also differs from the industrial Italian brands, which import wheat from Canada and Ukraine, among other distant sources. Each package of Pastificio dei Campi features geocoordinates for the fields on the Puglia-Campania border where the grain for Giuseppe's pasta is harvested every summer. That means wherever you are, eating Pastificio dei Campi pasta is a ticket directly to the flavors of the south.

CICATIELLI
CON *PULIEIO*

Cavatelli with Tomato and Wild Mint Pesto

Serves 4 to 6

---

4 garlic cloves

Sea salt

1½ cups loosely packed fresh *pulieio* (wild spearmint) or mint

1½ cups loosely packed fresh basil or parsley

7 tablespoons extra-virgin olive oil

1 teaspoon *peperoncino* or red pepper flakes

1 (14-ounce) can whole tomatoes, crushed by hand

1 cup Roma tomatoes, halved

1 pound fresh *cicatielli* (see page 90) or dried *cavatelli*

Chile oil (optional)

Pulieio in dialect—*puleggio* in Italian—is a wild herb from the Irpinia subregion of Campania. It's similar to mint, but with a more intense and persistent flavor and aroma. Locally, it's used for both medicine and food thanks to its digestive and anti-inflammatory properties. Here this tomato-enriched *pulieio* pesto dish is a terrific reminder that in Irpinia, food doesn't just provide sustenance—it's seen as medicine, a fact that is reinforced by the menthol and balsamic notes of the sauce. If you can't get your hands on *pulieio,* fresh mint (the wilder, the better) makes a fine substitute.

In a mortar, crush the garlic and a heavy pinch of salt into a paste with the pestle. Begin adding the mint and basil little by little. Add a bit of olive oil, but only as much as the herbs need in order to hydrate into a paste, no more than 3 tablespoons. If you add too much oil, the pesto will quickly turn from green to a blackish-olive color.

Heat the remaining 4 tablespoons olive oil in a large pan over medium heat. When the oil begins to shimmer, add the pesto and cook, stirring frequently, for several minutes. Add the *peperoncino* and cook until fragrant, about 30 seconds. Add the canned and Roma tomatoes, season with salt, and simmer until the tomatoes begin to fall apart and the sauce begins to thicken, about 25 minutes.

Meanwhile, bring a large pot of water to a rolling boil over high heat. Heavily salt the water (see page 31). When the salt has dissolved, add the *cicatielli* and cook until they lose their raw flavor, about 3 minutes. Drain the *cicatielli,* reserving the pasta cooking water, and add the pasta to the sauce, mixing well. Adjust the consistency of the sauce with pasta cooking water as needed. Cook, stirring occasionally, until the sauce loosely clings to the pasta, about a minute. Season with salt. Serve immediately, drizzled with chile oil, if desired.

ORECCHIETTE CON *BURRATA*, *POMODORINI*, *E PESTO*

Orecchiette with *Burrata*, Tomatoes, and Almond Pesto

Serves 4 to 6

FOR THE ROASTED TOMATOES

1½ cups cherry tomatoes, halved

2 tablespoons extra-virgin olive oil

½ teaspoon dried oregano

Sea salt

FOR THE PESTO

¼ cup almonds, finely chopped

1 cup loosely packed fresh basil leaves, plus more for garnish

Sea salt

3 tablespoons extra-virgin olive oil, plus more as needed

2 tablespoons freshly grated Parmigiano-Reggiano

FOR THE PASTA

1 pound fresh *Orecchiette al Grano Arso* (page 102) or dried orecchiette

7 ounces *burrata di Andria*

There are few pairings on earth as magical as oven-roasted tomatoes and *burrata*, cream-drenched mozzarella curds sheathed in mozzarella skin. The name, which comes from the Italian word for "butter" (*burro*), is just as decadent. This cheese is never heated, and is rarely paired with more than one other ingredient: salted anchovies, shaved bottarga, roasted or sun-dried tomatoes. On rare—and delicious occasions—you will find it served with almond-basil pesto and tomatoes and tossed with pasta. This summer dish popular in Puglia respects the *burrata*'s integrity by applying only the heat that comes from the cooked pasta. I like to use a mix of red and yellow tomatoes for a nice color and flavor contrast. It's a room temperature dish best enjoyed with a view of the Adriatic Sea, not far from its origins in Andria.

Make the roasted tomatoes: Preheat the oven to 250°F.

In a medium bowl, combine the cherry tomatoes, olive oil, and dried oregano. Season with salt.

Transfer to a medium baking dish and roast until the tomatoes are shriveled and dry, about 90 minutes.

Meanwhile, make the pesto: In a mortar, crush the almonds, ¼ cup of the basil, and a heavy pinch of salt into a paste with the pestle. Add a bit of olive oil, but only as much as the herbs need in order to hydrate into a paste, no more than 3 tablespoons. If you add too much oil, the pesto will quickly turn from green to a blackish-olive color. When you have a smooth paste, stir in the Parmigiano-Reggiano and set the pesto aside.

Cook the pasta: Bring a large pot of water to a rolling boil over high heat. Heavily salt the water (see page 31). When the salt has dissolved, add the orecchiette and cook until they lose their raw flavor, about 3 minutes. Drain the orecchiette and transfer to a large bowl. Add the pesto, stirring to coat. Stir in the tomatoes and the *burrata*. Plate and serve immediately, garnished with basil.

PACCHERI ALLA CILENTANA

Paccheri with Capers, Olives, Anchovies, and Fried Bread Crumbs

Serves 4 to 6

¼ cup extra-virgin olive oil, plus more to finish

2 garlic cloves, thinly sliced

4 salted anchovy fillets, cleaned (see page 134)

¾ cup Gaeta olives, rinsed and pitted

3 tablespoons capers, rinsed

Sea salt

1 pound *paccheri*

½ cup *Pane Grattugiato Fritto* (fried seasoned bread crumbs; page 107), for serving

---

The first time I drove along Cilento's Tyrrhenian Coast, I was astounded by the natural spectacle of the place. Caper plants clung to sheer cliffs around one turn, while the next revealed olive orchards teetering on impossibly vertical terraced farmland. Cilento's verdant beauty is occasionally interrupted by a tiny village where fishermen cast their nets into some of Italy's most pristine waters, raising wriggling anchovies from the Tyrrhenian Sea. After many visits to the Amalfi Coast, which is just a one-hour drive north of Cilento, it's impossible to not be floored by how unspoiled certain areas of Campania remain, totally untouched by the mass tourism and cruise ship itineraries that shape the Amalfi Coast today. This pasta dish is an homage to Campania's most unspoiled coastline, where olives and capers grow beside a sea teeming with anchovies. The tube-like *paccheri* "scoop" up all the savory sauce.

Heat the olive oil in a large skillet over low heat. When the oil begins to shimmer, add the garlic and anchovies and cook until the garlic begins to turn golden and the anchovies have melted into the oil, about 2 minutes. Add the olives and capers and cook, stirring, for 1 minute more. Turn off the heat and let the ingredients bloom in the hot oil.

Meanwhile, bring a large pot of water to a rolling boil over high heat. Salt the water (see page 31). When the salt has dissolved, add the *paccheri* and cook until al dente (see page 32). Drain the *paccheri,* reserving the pasta cooking water, and add the pasta to the pan with the olives and capers, stirring to coat. Add some pasta cooking water as needed to loosen the sauce. Season with salt to taste. Plate and sprinkle each portion with the fried seasoned bread crumbs and drizzle with olive oil.

NOTE I cannot overstate the importance of using high-quality olives. With the south's super-simple recipes, each flavor is conspicuous—the reason such basic recipes are so good is that they rely on ingredients at their peak. In Italy, it's not a luxury to have a family olive grove. It's not as common as it once was, but plenty of home cooks still have access to hand-harvested and naturally cured olives. So short of moving to Italy and befriending a farmer or buying a country house, invest in the best-quality olives you can afford. Avoid canned or presliced olives. If you don't have a good Italian deli in your neighborhood, look for purveyors of Greek, Turkish, North African, or Middle Eastern foods. If you can only find seasoned olives, rinse them before using, or cure your own (see page 50).

ORECCHIETTE *AL* GRANO ARSO

(Toasted-Flour
Orecchiette)

Makes about 1 pound

320 grams (2½ cups) *farina di semola*
(durum wheat flour; see page 203),
plus more as needed

1 cup plus 2 tablespoons warm water

Semolina, for dusting

Orecchiette, ear-shaped pasta, is a classic pasta type in Puglia where durum wheat grows and is milled into flour for use in cooking and baking. Local legend states that as the region was becoming industrialized, starving peasants would take to the fields after large mechanical combines had harvested the grain, collecting little burned bits of durum that the machine had left in its wake. More accurately, fields would be burned at the end of the season, and hungry farmers would harvest the bits of charred grain and mill this so-called *grano arso* (burned grain) to make flour for pasta.

Preheat the oven to 350°F.

Place 1 cup (130 grams) of the flour on a rimmed baking sheet, distributing it evenly in a thin layer. Toast the flour in the oven until golden and nearly smoking, about 35 minutes. Set aside to cool for about 5 minutes.

In a medium bowl, combine the toasted flour with the remaining 1½ cups (190 grams) flour.

Pour the flour mixture onto a work surface and make a well in the middle. Add the water, then mix with a fork, working from the edges of the well into the center, gradually incorporating it into the flour to form a shaggy dough. The dough should feel tacky but not sticky. If the dough sticks to your fingers, add 2 tablespoons more flour.

Knead the dough energetically until it is a smooth, compact mass, 10 to 12 minutes. Wrap the dough in plastic wrap and allow to rest at room temperature for 30 minutes before shaping. (At this point, the raw, unshaped dough can be tightly wrapped in plastic wrap and stored in the refrigerator for up to 1 week; it does not freeze well.)

When the dough has rested, flatten it into a disc about ½ inch thick. Cut off a strip of dough about ½ inch wide. Follow the instructions for shaping orecchiette (page 90).

The shaped pasta can be tightly wrapped in plastic wrap and frozen for up to a week.

Bring a large pot of water to a rolling boil over high heat. Heavily salt the water (see page 31). When the salt has dissolved, add the pasta and cook until the raw bite is gone, about 3 minutes. Serve with *Burrata, Pomodorini, e Pesto* (page 98) or the condiment of your choice.

FILJIE
CON RAGÙ
CALABRESE

Fusilli with
Calabrian-Style
Pork *Ragù*

Serves 4 to 6

---

2 tablespoons lard

1 pound pork spareribs, cut into 2-inch pieces or whole, salted in advance

3½ ounces pancetta, diced (¾ cup)

2 onions, diced

2 celery stalks, diced

2 carrots, diced

1 teaspoon freshly grated nutmeg

Sea salt

¼ cup tomato paste

1 cup dry red wine (I like Cirò)

1 (28-ounce) cans whole tomatoes, crushed by hand

1 pound fresh *filjie* (see page 92) or dried fusilli

½ cup finely grated Parmigiano-Reggiano

Whole fresh *peperoncino* (see page 37) or chile oil

NOTE In South Italy, many sauces feature meat on the bone, which means you're encouraged to pick up the meat with your fingers to polish it off. If you prefer a more refined (but perhaps less exciting) approach, pick the meat off the bone when the pork is tender and stir it back into the sauce; discard the bones.

Ragù is a loaded word—like so much food terminology, its meaning depends on where you are and to whom you're talking. Mention *ragù* in Naples, and the word conjures a viscous sauce made with onions, lard, beef, pork, and tomato. In the Sannio, *ragù* is made from mutton simmered in tomato sauce. Meanwhile, throughout Calabria, *ragù* denotes a pork-driven tomato-based sauce. Of course there's lard in this Calabrian-style *ragù*; fat and flavor sources for villages 850 meters above sea level remains pork to this day. The pasta is often served with a side of personal *peperoncino,* a single fresh chile pepper and a knife for each diner, so guests can regulate the heat of their own dishes. This recipe makes 1½ quarts of *ragù*, plenty for serving four to six people with sauce left over, which you can freeze. Salt the ribs 24 hours in advance.

Melt the lard in a large pot over medium-high heat. When the fat begins to shimmer, add the ribs and cook, turning occasionally, until browned, about 10 minutes, then remove the ribs and set aside. Reduce the heat to medium, add the pancetta, and cook until the fat has rendered, about 10 minutes. Add the onions, celery, carrots, nutmeg, and a pinch of salt. Cook until the vegetables are soft and the onions are translucent, 15 to 20 minutes. Add the tomato paste and cook until it turns a deep brick red, about 2 minutes. Add the wine, scraping up any bits stuck to the bottom of the pan, and cook until the alcohol aroma dissipates, 2 to 4 minutes. Add the tomatoes and ribs and enough water to cover, then season with salt. Reduce the heat to low and simmer until the pork is fork-tender, 1 to 2 hours. Keep the pork at least halfway submerged, adding water as needed.

Check for doneness frequently after the 1-hour mark. When a toothpick or fork easily goes through the meat, it is cooked. Season with salt.

Meanwhile, bring a large pot of water to a rolling boil over high heat. Heavily salt the water (see page 31). When the salt has dissolved, add the *filjie* and cook until they lose their raw flavor, about 3 minutes. Drain the *filjie,* reserving the pasta cooking water, and add the pasta to the *ragù*, stirring to coat. Add some pasta cooking water to loosen the sauce as needed. Cook, stirring occasionally, until the sauce loosely clings to the pasta, about 1 minute. Season with salt. Serve immediately, with Parmigiano-Reggiano sprinkled on top and fresh *peperoncino* on the side.

'O SCARPARIELLO

Spaghetti with Garlic and
Corbara Tomatoes

Serves 4 to 6

½ cup extra-virgin olive oil

2 garlic cloves, smashed

1 teaspoon *peperoncino* or red pepper
flakes

1 pound Corbara, San Marzano,
or ripe plum tomatoes, roughly
chopped

5 or 6 basil leaves, plus more for
garnish

Sea salt

1 pound *spaghettoni* or spaghetti

San Marzano tomatoes might have the best publicity—
they have become by far the best known (and
incidentally the most counterfeited) Italian tomatoes.
Plenty of other varieties grow near Mount Vesuvius
that are worth seeking out, including Corbara
tomatoes. Named for the town around which they
grow, these tomatoes thrive in the fields overlooking
the Bay of Naples and the Agro Nocerino area. If
you don't, say, live on the slopes of Mount Vesuvius
with easy access to fresh Corbara tomatoes, you can
substitute bottled whole Corbara tomatoes or ripe plum
tomatoes.

Use the pasta cooking water to your advantage
to help the sauce cling to the pasta. The starchy water
emulsifies with the oil in the tomato sauce to create a
slightly creamy texture and glossy consistency.

Heat the olive oil in a large skillet over low heat. When
the oil begins to shimmer, add the garlic and cook until it
just turns golden, about 5 minutes. Add the *peperoncino*
and cook until fragrant, about 30 seconds. Discard the
garlic, or leave it in (Neapolitans do either), then add the
tomatoes and basil, season with salt, and cook until the
tomatoes are very soft, about 20 minutes.

Meanwhile, bring a large pot of water to a rolling boil
over high heat. Salt the water (see page 31). When the
salt has dissolved, add the *spaghettoni* and cook until
very al dente (see page 32). Drain the *spaghettoni,*
reserving the pasta cooking water, and add the pasta
to the tomato sauce, stirring to coat. Add ¼ cup of
the pasta cooking water to sauce, increase the heat
to medium, and simmer, stirring vigorously, until the
pasta is al dente. Add a bit more pasta cooking water to
loosen the sauce as needed.

Plate and serve immediately, garnished with basil.

RASCHIATELLI
ALLA MOLLICA

Pasta with
Fried Bread Crumbs

Serves 4 to 6

3 tablespoons extra-virgin olive oil

1 garlic clove, smashed

1 *peperoncino* or 1 teaspoon red
pepper flakes

Sea salt

1 pound fresh *raschiatelli* (see page 90),
dried *cavatelli*, or spaghetti

2 cups *Pane Grattugiato Fritto*
(recipe follows)

Italians aren't known for having a wild drinking culture—leave that to Anglo-Americans on holiday—but after a night out dancing, it's not unheard of to come home a little buzzed. Pasta with fried bread crumbs is the south's go-to drunk food. It's simple to whip up with ingredients everyone has in their pantry; just combine pasta with garlic-and-chile-infused oil and top with seasoned bread crumbs.

Heat the olive oil in a large skillet over medium-low heat. When the oil begins to shimmer, add the garlic and cook until it turns golden, about 5 minutes. Add the *peperoncino* and cook until fragrant, about 30 seconds.

Meanwhile, bring a large pot of water to a rolling boil over high heat. Heavily salt the water (see page 31). When the salt has dissolved, add the *raschiatelli* and cook until they lose their raw flavor, about 3 minutes. Drain the *raschiatelli,* reserving the pasta cooking water, and add the pasta to the pan with the oil, stirring to coat. Add some pasta cooking water to loosen the sauce as needed. Cook, stirring occasionally, until the oil loosely clings to the pasta, about a minute. Season with salt. Serve immediately, with *Pane Grattugiato Fritto* sprinkled on top.

Pane Grattugiato Fritto
Fried Bread Crumbs
Makes 2 cups

"Frying" the bread crumbs in the oven instead of a frying pan helps them stay crispy.

8 to 10 slices dry rustic
bread with crusts, torn
into bite-size pieces

¼ cup extra-virgin
olive oil

2 teaspoons dried oregano
or chopped fresh flat-leaf
parsley

Sea salt

Preheat the oven to 250°F.

In a large bowl, toss the bread, olive oil, oregano, and salt until well combined. Spread out the bread pieces on a rimmed baking sheet and bake until crispy and completely dried out, 15 to 20 minutes. Remove from the oven and allow to cool. Transfer to a food processor and pulse until broken down to the size of coarse coffee grounds.

Store in an airtight container at room temperature for up to 2 days.

Cultura Arbëreshë
Arbëreshë Culture

As you drive along the coastal road between the Pugliese towns of Lecce and Otranto, turn on your radio and run through the stations. Between the Italian broadcasts, you'll catch some waves sailing across the Adriatic Sea from Albania. It's easy to forget how close the Balkans are from the heel of Italy's boot, just forty-five miles at the closest point. It's this proximity, coupled with historic ties between Albanian nobility and Italian kingdoms, that has led Albanians to Italy as refugees for the last five centuries.

Between the fifteenth and seventeenth centuries, as Ottoman forces conquered the Balkans, many Albanians escaped to South Italy, founding nearly one hundred villages in Calabria, Basilicata, Puglia, and Molise. The first refugees arrived in Italy in the late 1400s following the uprising and guerilla war that Albanian general Gjergj Kastrioti, known as Skanderbeg, waged against the Ottomans after defecting from their ranks. Skanderbeg negotiated a treaty with Aragon King Alfonso I of Naples under which he and his men would be vassals for Spain's territories in Southern Italy. Over the third quarter of the fifteenth century, Skanderbeg traveled between Albania and Italy, battling against the Ottomans in the former, while fighting to secure Aragon sovereignty in the latter. After Skanderbeg's death, King Ferdinand I issued a decree accepting Albanians into his kingdom, thus heralding the arrival of thousands of refugees in Italy.

Today, the majority of Albanian, or Arbëreshë, communities in Italy are clustered in Calabria and Basilicata. Perhaps the best known is Civita. Set between two peaks in a dramatic valley created by a now dried-up river, the village is the center of Arbëreshë life in the surrounding area. There are a pair of restaurants off the main square as well as the butcher shop and a deli selling typical Arbëreshë items. Most of the signage is bilingual Italian/Arbëreshë, but unless you are in town for *Java e Madhe* (Holy Week) or the springtime *Le Vallje* festival commemorating a historic Albanian battle, when locals dress in traditional garb and speak their fifteenth-century southern Albanian dialect, you might not notice the unique Arbëreshë cultural distinctions.

At Civita's restaurants Agorà and Kamastra, you will find local specialties like *rrashkatjel me mish derku* (*ferretto*-rolled pasta with pork *ragù*), *kangariqra kothra e ve* (eggs with salami), and *dromësat* (a shaggy couscous-like pasta cooked in tomato broth). These, like so many Arbëreshë dishes, remain distinctly linked to this unique culture, while also showing the influence of their Calabrian surroundings through the use of local herbs and the techniques of handmade pasta.

SPAGHETTI CON COLATURA DI ALICI

Spaghetti with Anchovy Sauce

Serves 4 to 6

¼ cup extra-virgin olive oil

1 garlic clove, smashed

6 sprigs plus 2 tablespoons packed roughly chopped fresh parsley

Sea salt

1 pound *spaghettoni* or spaghetti

Colatura di Alici (see page 125)

This dish is one of my favorites to whip up when I have almost nothing left in the cupboard except the bare necessities (yes, in Italy, *colatura*, a traditional fish sauce, is a standard pantry item). This pungent liquid, made from fermented anchovies, is rich in fishy umami. In Cetara, the town on the Amalfi Coast where the most famous *colatura* is made, some don't cook the oil, garlic, or parsley at all, allowing the hot pasta to do all the work; others sizzle the aforementioned ingredients over low heat. *Cetaresi* are in universal agreement, however, that *colatura* should never be cooked, as it takes on an unpleasant flavor when heated, so be sure to add it off the heat. If you're a newbie to the wonderfully fishy world of *colatura*, add just a few drops at a time to taste.

Heat the olive oil in large pan over medium-low heat. When the oil begins to shimmer, add the garlic and cook until fragrant, about 2 minutes. Add the parsley sprigs and cook until fragrant, about 30 seconds.

Meanwhile, bring a large pot of water to a rolling boil over high heat. Salt the water (see page 31). When the salt has dissolved, add the *spaghettoni* and cook until very al dente (see page 32). Drain the *spaghettoni*, reserving the pasta cooking water, and add the pasta and 1 cup of the pasta cooking water to the sauce, stirring to coat. Increase the heat to medium-high and stir until most of the water has been absorbed. Add a bit more pasta cooking water to loosen the sauce as needed. Remove the pan from the heat.

Add *colatura* to taste, garnish with the chopped parsley, and toss well. Serve immediately.

CANDELE CON 'NDUJA

Candele with 'Nduja

Serves 4 to 6

---

2 tablespoons extra-virgin olive oil

1 onion, diced

Sea salt

4 ounces *'nduja*

1 (14-ounce) can whole tomatoes, crushed by hand

1 pound dried *candele* or smooth ziti, or fresh *filjie* (see page 92)

2 ounces *ricotta salata*, coarsely grated

It's almost always sacrilege to break pasta before boiling it, but as with all things Italian, there are exceptions to the rule. *Candele* are two-foot-long (or longer) tubes of pasta that must be broken before being cooked—otherwise, they won't fit in the pot. You will find them served with thick, fatty *ragù* in northern Campania, while down the peninsula in Calabria, they are dressed with viscous *'nduja* sauce. *'Nduja* is a spreadable Calabrian pork salami spiked with fermented chile. There's quite a bit more fat in Calabrian *'nduja* than in American versions like those made by La Quercia and Chicago-based 'Nduja Artisans (see Resources, page 248), so expect it to be a touch lighter than its Calabrian counterpart. If you can't find *candele*, substitute smooth ziti. You can also serve this dish with *filjie* (see page 92).

Heat the olive oil in a large skillet over medium-low heat. When the oil begins to shimmer, add the onion, season with salt, and cook until soft and translucent, about 15 minutes. Add the *'nduja* and stir until all the fatty bits have melted, about 4 minutes. Add the tomatoes and cook until the sauce thickens and the tomatoes have lost their raw flavor, about 15 minutes. Simmer for a few minutes more to allow the flavors to marry.

Meanwhile, bring a large pot of water to a rolling boil over high heat. Salt the water (see page 31). When the salt has dissolved, break the *candele* into approximately 3-inch pieces and cook until al dente (see page 32). Drain the *candele,* reserving the pasta cooking water, and add the pasta and ¼ cup of the pasta cooking water to the sauce, stirring well to coat. Add a bit more pasta cooking water to loosen the sauce as needed.

Serve immediately, with the *ricotta salata* sprinkled on top.

NOTE The USDA strictly prohibits importing *'nduja* directly from Italy, but if you're willing to risk a fine and possible incineration of your fatty meat spread, grab some at fine delis (look for Romano brand) and have it vacuum packed for your transatlantic flight. I'm not encouraging you to violate the law, but I'm also not *not* endorsing a bit of meat smuggling.

SICCHIE D'A MUNNEZZA

Spaghetti with Dried
Fruits and Nuts

Serves 4 to 6

⅓ cup extra-virgin olive oil

2 garlic cloves, smashed

⅓ cup walnuts, roughly chopped

⅓ cup hazelnuts, roughly chopped

⅓ cup pine nuts

1 tablespoon chopped fresh flat-leaf
parsley

½ (14-ounce) can whole tomatoes
crushed by hand

¼ cup Gaeta olives, rinsed, pitted,
and roughly chopped

¼ cup capers, rinsed and roughly
chopped

¼ cup raisins

Sea salt

2 teaspoons dried oregano

1 pound *spaghettoni* or spaghetti

Sicchie d'a munnezza, which translates to "garbage can,"
doesn't exactly conjure thoughts of deliciousness, but
I assure you this Christmas-season dish is super tasty.
The ingredients, a potpourri of scraps like dried fruits
and nuts that might be left over from the preparation of
a savory and sweet feast, are simmered in oil and tossed
with spaghetti in the town of Sant'Anastasia near Mount
Vesuvius. It's the signature dish at 'E Curti, where cook
Angela Ceriello prepares it in warped aluminum pans
in her cavernous kitchen all year long. If you stop by, be
sure to ask Angela for a peek at her collection of copper
pots, and don't forget to wrap up the meal with *Nucillo*
(page 244), their homemade walnut liqueur.

Heat the olive oil in a large skillet over low heat. When
the oil begins to shimmer, add the garlic and cook until
it turns golden, about 5 minutes. Add the walnuts,
hazelnuts, and pine nuts and cook until the pine nuts
begin to color, about 5 minutes. Add the parsley and
cook until fragrant, about 30 seconds, then add the
tomatoes, olives, capers, and raisins and season with
salt. Simmer until the tomatoes have reduced slightly
and lost their raw flavor, about 15 minutes, then add the
oregano. Season with salt.

Meanwhile, bring a large pot of water to a rolling boil
over high heat. Salt the water (see page 31). When the
salt has dissolved, add the *spaghettoni* and cook until
al dente (see page 32). Drain the *spaghettoni,* reserving
the pasta cooking water, and add the pasta and ¼ cup
of the pasta cooking water to the sauce, stirring to
coat. Add a bit more pasta cooking water to loosen the
sauce as needed. Serve immediately.

PESCE

—

FISH

CAURARO

Anchovy and Spring
Vegetable Stew

Serves 4 to 6

¼ cup extra-virgin olive oil

1 large onion, chopped

1 garlic clove, smashed

2 salted anchovy fillets, cleaned
(see page 134)

½ bunch wild fennel, roughly chopped

2 cups chopped dandelion greens

2 cups chopped beet greens or
Swiss chard

1 cup halved new potatoes

1 cup peeled shelled fava beans

Sea salt and freshly ground black
pepper

½ pound fresh anchovies, cleaned
and filleted

Anchovies from Cetara on the Amalfi Coast may be the most famous anchovies in Italy, but in-the-know fish lovers travel seventy miles farther south to Pisciotta for fish caught in the pristine waters off Cilento's coast. At Angiolina, this fisherman's dish, which actually relies more on vegetables and wild fennel than on fish, features anchovies in a supporting role in both salted and fresh form. Directly in front of the restaurant, the Tyrrhenian Sea stretches westward to the horizon, and it is in these waters that Pisciotta's few remaining fishermen catch anchovies in special nets called *menaiche*, which have wide openings. Locals credit the ancient Greeks for introducing *menaiche* to their shores and recount that the net's sustainable design guarantees that only fish above reproductive age are snared.

Heat the olive oil in a large pot over medium-low heat. When the oil begins to shimmer, add the onion, garlic, and anchovy fillets. Cook until the garlic just begins to turn golden and the anchovy fillets break down and melt into the oil, about 5 minutes. Add the fennel and cook until fragrant, 1 minute more.

Add the dandelion greens, beet greens, potatoes, and favas. Add enough water to cover. Season with salt and bring to a simmer. Reduce the heat to low and simmer until the potatoes are cooked through, about 30 minutes.

Lay the fresh anchovies over the vegetables, season with salt and pepper, cover, and simmer until the fish are opaque and cooked through, about 3 minutes. Serve immediately, ladled into shallow bowls.

COZZE RIPIENE

Stuffed Mussels

Serves 4 to 6

1 pound mussels (about 25),
  beards removed and scrubbed
  (see page 134)

2 cups fresh bread crumbs

2 eggs, beaten

3 ounces (about half a can) tuna in oil,
  drained

¼ cup finely grated Pecorino Romano

2 tablespoons chopped fresh flat-leaf
  parsley

Sea salt and freshly ground black
  pepper

2 cups cherry tomatoes, halved

3 tablespoons extra-virgin olive oil

Puglia's coastline is lapped by two seas—the Adriatic and the Ionian, both of which are chronically overfished, leaving shellfish and crustaceans among the few reasonably sustainable options. *Pugliesi* eat mussels in many forms, and there are even many variations on the stuffed mussel—in most of the region, they are packed with seasoned bread crumbs and deep-fried. This version is from Salento, the "heel" of the Italian boot. It takes a lighter approach, instead baking the mussels with tomatoes to sort of steam them in their shells. Double the recipe to serve as a main dish; otherwise, *cozze ripiene* are a perfect companion to *Insalata di Polpo con le Patate* (page 133) and *Scapece alla Gallipolina* (page 127) in a fish-based *antipasto* spread.

Preheat the oven to 400°F.

Using a dull knife, open the mussels (see page 134), working over a large bowl to catch their liquid. Set aside the open mussels.

Add the bread crumbs, eggs, tuna, Pecorino Romano, and parsley to the bowl with the mussel liquid. Mix well to combine. The mixture should be wet but not runny; add a bit of water if needed. Season with salt and pepper. (The ingredients are already quite savory, so you may not need any salt.)

Using your hands, place about a tablespoon of the bread crumb mixture in each open mussel, gently closing the mussel around the filling but allowing some of the filling to spill over.

Arrange the filled mussels evenly inside a large baking dish.

In a small bowl, combine the tomatoes, 2 to 3 tablespoons water, and the olive oil. Season with salt and toss to coat. Distribute the tomatoes evenly around the mussels. Bake until the filling is browned and the tomatoes are softened, 20 to 25 minutes. Switch the oven to broil and broil for 5 minutes to get a light golden crust on the bread crumb filling. Serve at room temperature.

PESCE SPADA ALLA SCILLANESE

Swordfish Rolls

Serves 6 to 8

6 tablespoons extra-virgin olive oil

1 garlic clove, smashed

6 sprigs plus 3 tablespoons finely
   chopped fresh flat-leaf parsley

1 teaspoon *peperoncino* or
   red pepper flakes

5 cups mature cherry tomatoes, halved

Sea salt

3 cups *Pane Grattugiato* (seasoned
   bread crumbs; recipe follows)

½ cup finely grated Pecorino Romano

¼ cup capers, rinsed and roughly
   chopped

¼ cup diced olives, rinsed

3 pounds swordfish, skin removed,
   cut into ¼-inch-thick slices about
   2 × 4 inches

Nearly at the Strait of Messina, the narrow strip of water that separates mainland Italy from Sicily, the town of Scilla is home to a historic swordfish industry. Scilla's seaside district of Chianalea overlooks a small harbor that was once filled with *passarelle* (runways), the typical swordfish fishing vessels so-called for their 150-foot-long prow. For centuries, fishermen ventured into the turbulent seas to catch swordfish, which they spotted from the *passarella's* lookout tower attached to the mast. The catch was sold as steaks, smeared with a stuffing studded with capers that grew wild on Scilla's stone walls, then rolled into *involtini*.

Heat 2 tablespoons of the olive oil in a large skillet over medium-low heat. When the oil begins to shimmer, add the garlic and cook until it just turns golden, about 5 minutes. Add the parsley sprigs and *peperoncino* and cook until fragrant, about 30 seconds. Add the cherry tomatoes, season with salt, and cook until softened, about 10 minutes.

Meanwhile, in a medium bowl, combine the bread crumbs, Pecorino Romano, capers, olives, remaining 4 tablespoons olive oil, 2 tablespoons of the chopped parsley, and a few tablespoons of water, or enough to form a thick paste.

Lay the swordfish slices flat on your work surface and season with salt on both sides. Divide the bread crumb mixture evenly over swordfish fillets. Roll the fish around the filling, forming medium-tight *involtini*. Use kitchen twine or a couple of toothpicks inserted flush with the fish to keep the rolls closed.

Add the *involtini* to the pan with the tomato sauce, increase the heat to medium, and cook, covered, until the fish is opaque and slightly firm to the touch, about 10 minutes. Add a bit of water to the pan before adding the fish if the sauce seems dry.

Serve immediately, garnished with the remaining 1 tablespoon chopped parsley.

NOTE If you do not have kitchen twine or toothpicks, roll up the *involtini* tightly and place them snugly next to one another in a smaller pan.

Pane Grattugiato

Seasoned Bread Crumbs

Makes 3 cups

12 to 15 slices dry rustic bread, with
   crusts, torn into bite-size pieces

4 teaspoons dried oregano or chopped
   fresh flat-leaf parsley

¼ cup finely grated Pecorino
   Romano, Parmigiano-Reggiano,
   or Grana Padano

Preheat the oven to 250°F.

Spread out the bread pieces on a rimmed baking sheet
and bake until crispy and completely dried out, 15 to
20 minutes.

Remove from the oven and allow to cool. Transfer to a
food processor and pulse until broken down to the size
of coarse coffee grounds.

Transfer the bread crumbs to a medium bowl, add the
oregano and grated cheese, and mix thoroughly.

Store in an airtight container at room temperature for
up to 1 week.

Vigilia di Natale
Christmas Eve

In Italy, there's no such thing as the Feast of the Seven Fishes, the popular Christmas Eve meal enjoyed by many Italian American families. Somehow, the *Vigilia di Natale*, the December 24 fish bonanza, got whittled down when it reached American shores. In the south, serving a mere seven fishes would be sacrilege—snag an invite to a Christmas Eve dinner for proof, and if you can, get in on the days of prep that go into this elaborate holiday meal.

The reason for eating fish for the *Vigilia* is, naturally, related to the Catholic Church, which used to mandate lean, meatless meals on sacred holidays. Although these rules have loosened considerably, the custom of eating fish on Catholic holidays has stuck around. Today, however, the concept of eating moderately on those days has vanished, and instead, families go all out, serving a huge amount of food and many dishes for the purpose of celebration rather than solemnity.

In Bari, Puglia's largest city, Christmas Eve starts with a lavish spread of *crudi* (raw fish), and crustaceans like oysters, *cozze pellose* (the local "hairy" mussel), *tartufi di mare* (meaty warty Venus clams), followed by *Insalata di Polpo con le Patate* (page 133), baked scallops, fried *baccalà*, spaghetti with seafood, and whole baked and fried fish and eels.

In Reggio Calabria, *zeppole alle acciughe* (anchovy-studded fritters), are a typical starter, while in Naples, the classic Christmas Eve dishes

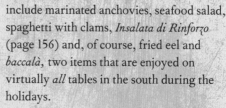

include marinated anchovies, seafood salad, spaghetti with clams, *Insalata di Rinforzo* (page 156) and, of course, fried eel and *baccalà*, two items that are enjoyed on virtually *all* tables in the south during the holidays.

Regardless of where it's celebrated, you'll be impressed by how moderate the Feast of the Seven Fishes seems by comparison.

ALICI ARRAGANATE

Pan-Fried Anchovies

Serves 4 to 6

½ cup extra-virgin olive oil

2 garlic cloves, smashed

1 *peperoncino* or 1 teaspoon red pepper flakes

2 pounds whole fresh anchovies, cleaned (see page 134)

5 sprigs plus 1 tablespoon packed chopped fresh flat-leaf parsley

Sea salt

2 lemons, quartered

Alici arraganate is one of the many dishes in the south that varies wildly depending on where you are. Between southern Abruzzo and northern Puglia, it's a breaded anchovy casserole, while on the other side of the peninsula in Calabria, it's a piping-hot and piquant dish of pan-fried anchovies. *Calabresi* crave heat, but only by Italian standards, so the spiciness of their chiles is moderate compared to your conventional spicy chile in the United States. Feel free to use the pepper of your choice.

The key to this dish is to use a very hot pan and a good amount of oil—skimping on heat or fat here will result in a fishy mess. When you increase the heat to high, the garlic and *peperoncino* may begin to burn. That's all right—it's actually quite common for dishes from the south to feature browned garlic and charred *peperoncino*.

Heat the olive oil in a large pan over medium heat. When the oil begins to shimmer, add the garlic and cook until it just begins to take color, about 5 minutes. Add the *peperoncino* and cook until fragrant, about 30 seconds.

Increase the heat to high and add the anchovies and parsley sprigs (work in batches as needed). Season with salt. Cook until the anchovies are cooked through and slightly firm to the touch, turning once to ensure even cooking, about 1 minute. Serve immediately, with the chopped parsley sprinkled on top and lemon on the side.

Colatura di Alici
Anchovy Sauce

Colatura di alici, a pungent anchovy sauce, is often erroneously called garum, which was an ancient condiment made from fermented anchovies and their entrails. The word comes from *garos*, a type of fish the Greeks used to make *liquamen*, or fermented fish sauce, as early as the fifth century BC. By the time Pliny the Elder was writing about it in the first century AD, the Romans had codified the recipe. In *Natural History XXXI.93*, Pliny wrote that garum consisted of "the guts of fish and the other parts that would otherwise be considered refuse; these are soaked in salt, so that garum is really liquor from the putrefaction of these matters."

The custom of fermenting small fish like mullets, sardines, and anchovies was practiced throughout the Mediterranean in ancient times, and their sauces made around Pompeii were particularly prized. After the fall of the empire, garum production ground to a halt, but in the Middle Ages, Cistercian monks near the Amalfi Coast "accidentally" invented a simpler but no less flavorful version. Local lore states that some monks lost track of a barrel of salted anchovies in their cellar. When they found it, years later, the liquid that had risen to the top of the barrel was so abundant, they thought it was sinful to waste it, and so *colatura di alici* was born.

Today, the capital of *colatura* production is Cetara, a small fishing village near the southern edge of the Amalfi Coast. Shops, restaurants, and *laboratori* situated around the village produce and sell their own *colatura*. At Nettuno, my favorite *colatura* workshop, it takes up to three years to produce the savory liquid. There, anchovies and salt are dutifully layered by hand in wooden barrels, then set aside with weighted lids. The fish slowly exude their liquid, which is collected and bottled only after owner Giulio Giordano has judged it is just right. On one recent trip, as we sat together in his workshop, he laughed off *colatura*'s connection to garum, declaring his concoction a far more elegant product. Each time I use his *colatura*, more often than not for making *Spaghetti con Colatura di Alici* (page 110), I marvel at Giulio's quite justified claim that such humble ingredients can make something so precious.

SCAPECE ALLA GALLIPOLINA

Fried Marinated Sardines
with Saffron

Serves 4 to 6

1 cup white wine vinegar

¼ cup water

6 to 8 saffron threads

Neutral oil (see page 37), for frying

1 cup all-purpose flour

2 pounds whole fresh sardines, cleaned
(see page 134)

Sea salt

The custom of frying fish or vegetables, then preserving them in vinegar is an ancient tradition practiced throughout South Italy and indeed the world. The term *scapece* derives from the Spanish *escabesche*, a pickling method. In Gallipoli, a wind-wizened, labyrinthine city on Puglia's Ionian coast, fishermen catch sardines, which are fried and packed in wooden containers with vinegar, saffron, and bread crumbs. This recipe has been modified to exclude the bread crumbs—and accordingly, the strange, pulpy texture they impart—which I think tastes a lot better.

In a small saucepan, combine the vinegar and water and heat over low heat. Just before it boils, remove it from the heat and add the saffron. Set aside to bloom.

Meanwhile, line a baking sheet with paper towels.

In a medium frying pan or cast-iron skillet, heat 2 inches of oil to 350°F.

Place the flour in a shallow bowl. Dredge each sardine in flour, shaking off any excess.

Working in batches as needed, fry the sardines, turning once to ensure even cooking, just until golden, about 1 minute. Drain on paper towels and season with salt. Be sure the oil returns to 350°F before adding the next batch.

Layer the fish in a glass or ceramic dish. Pour the vinegar mixture over the fish. Cover and refrigerate for 2 to 3 days before serving.

NOTE If you don't have a thermometer, test the oil's readiness by dropping in a piece of bread. If it browns in about 60 seconds, the oil is hot enough for frying. Alternatively, put the end of a wooden spoon in the oil; if the oil bubbles around the spoon, it's hot enough.

SEPPIA SCKATTIATA

Cuttlefish Cooked in Oil

Serves 4 to 6

4 cuttlefish, cleaned (see page 134)

¼ cup extra-virgin olive oil

1 spring onion or scallion, chopped

1 garlic clove, smashed

Sea salt

1 tablespoon *peperoni cruschi* powder or sweet paprika

Trebisacce on Calabria's Ionian coast—Italy's "instep"—is a historic port for cuttlefish fishing. At their restaurant Da Lucrezia, Lucrezia Galia and her son Giuseppe Gatto serve the village's signature dish, *sckattiata*, cuttlefish cooked in a terra-cotta pot. As the cephalopod cooks, it sizzles and pops—*sckattiata* means "explosion" in the local dialect. The dish is seasoned with ground *peperoni cruschi*, fried sweet peppers typical of Senise just across the border in Basilicata, which lend a sweet and smoky note.

Place the cuttlefish in a medium pot and add water to cover. Simmer over low heat until the water has evaporated and the cuttlefish is tender, about 1 hour. Remove the cuttlefish from the pot and set aside to cool. When the cuttlefish is cool enough to handle, about 10 minutes, cut into bite-size pieces.

Add the olive oil to the same pot and increase the heat to medium. When the oil begins to shimmer, add the spring onion and garlic, season with salt, and cook until the garlic just begins to color, about 5 minutes. Return the cooked cuttlefish to the pot and stir well to coat. Add the *peperoni cruschi* and cook for 5 minutes more, until the flavors have married. Season with salt. Serve immediately.

U MORZEDDHU E BACCALÀ

Cod with Chile, Peppers, Tomato, and Paprika

Serves 4

⅔ cup extra-virgin olive oil

1 garlic clove, smashed

1 Tropea onion, diced

Sea salt

1 tablespoon sweet paprika

1 tablespoon *peperoncino* or red pepper flakes

¼ cup tomato paste

1 (14-ounce) can whole tomatoes, crushed by hand

1 pound salt cod fillets, desalted (see Note), rinsed, and cut into bite-size pieces

1 teaspoon dried oregano

Whole fresh *peperoncino* (optional)

U Ficcilatìdd (page 204), for serving

In the past, cauldrons of tripe stew would bubble in the kitchens of Catanzaro for hours, the aroma strong with oregano. On the lean days prescribed by the Catholic calendar, especially Fridays and during Lent, the tripe would be swapped out for *u morzeddhu e baccalà*, strips of salted cod. It was generally served in a *pitta*, a circular bread typical of the interior Calabrian town of Catanzaro. The cod was stuffed into the bread, which was then sliced into segments. It was a messy dish overflowing with sauce. When I can't get down to Catanzaro for *pitta*, I use a bread called *u ficcilatìdd*, which makes a great substitute.

Heat the olive oil in a medium saucepan over medium-low heat. When the oil begins to shimmer, add the garlic and onion, season with salt, and cook until the onion is soft and translucent, about 15 minutes. Add the paprika and *peperoncino* and cook until fragrant, about 30 seconds. Add the tomato paste and cook until it turns a deep brick red, about 2 minutes.

Add the tomatoes and cook for a couple of minutes, until they have lost their raw flavor, then add the cod and enough water to cover. Bring to a boil, add the oregano, reduce the heat to low, and simmer until the cod is tender and heated through, 5 to 10 minutes. Serve immediately on its own or as a sandwich filling with whole fresh *peperoncino* on the side.

NOTE To desalt the cod, cut it into equal pieces and soak in water in the refrigerator for at least 24 hours and up to 48 hours, changing the water at least four times, until the water (and therefore the fish) is no longer salty.

BRODETTO DI PESCE ALLA TERMOLESE

Termoli-Style Fish Soup

Serves 4 to 6

¼ cup extra-virgin olive oil

1 garlic clove, smashed

1 green bell pepper, diced

Sea salt

6 sprigs plus 2 tablespoons finely chopped fresh flat-leaf parsley

1 cup dry white wine

½ (14-ounce) can whole tomatoes, crushed by hand

1 cup water

½ pound clams, cleaned

½ pound mussels, beards removed and scrubbed (see page 134)

2½ pounds cleaned whole seafood, such as young red mullet, small scorpion fish, mantis shrimp, and cod (see page 134)

1 pound medium shrimp (shell and heads left on), deveined

½ pound calamari, sliced into rings

Locally called *u brudette,* this fish soup is from Termoli, a picture-perfect seaside village in the middle of Molise's brief thirty-mile coastline along the Adriatic. The region's traditional fishing instruments, called *trabocchi,* use a cantilever to project nets over the water and to raise and lower them into the sea. The nets are designed for small fish like the ones in this soup, which are accompanied by shellfish and green bell peppers. Osteria dentro le Mura, a cavernous trattoria in the historic old town, is a great spot to try Termoli's answer to bouillabaisse at the source.

Heat the olive oil in a large saucepan over medium-low heat. When the oil begins to shimmer, add the garlic and cook until it just turns golden, about 5 minutes. Add the bell pepper, season with salt, and cook until softened, about 5 minutes. Add the parsley sprigs and cook until fragrant, about 30 seconds. Add the wine and cook until the alcohol aroma dissipates, about 1 minute.

Add the tomatoes and bring to a simmer. Add the water and simmer for a few minutes more, until the tomatoes lose their raw flavor, then add the clams and mussels. Cover the pan and return to a simmer. When the clams and mussels start to open, add the fish fillets. Cover and reduce the heat to low to gently cook the fish halfway, about 2 minutes.

Add the shrimp and calamari, cover, and cook for 2 minutes more, or until the fish is opaque and tender when pierced with a fork but not flaking apart and the shrimp and calamari are opaque and tender.

Serve immediately in bowls and sprinkle with the chopped parsley.

INSALATA DI POLPO CON LE PATATE

Octopus and Potato Salad

Serves 4 to 6

2 pounds octopus, cleaned
(see page 134)

Zest of 1 lemon, removed with a
vegetable peeler

Zest of 1 orange, removed with a
vegetable peeler

1 tablespoon whole black peppercorns,
toasted and crushed

1 bay leaf

1 sprig fresh rosemary

1 small white onion, halved

1 cup dry white wine

1 pound new potatoes

¾ cup plus 1 tablespoon extra-virgin
olive oil, plus more as needed

3 tablespoons fresh lemon juice (from
1 lemon), plus more as needed

2 tablespoons fresh mint, finely
chopped

¼ cup finely chopped fresh flat-leaf
parsley

Freshly ground black pepper

½ cup Gaeta olives, rinsed, pitted,
and halved lengthwise

½ pound young green beans,
cut into 1-inch pieces

Sea salt

Thanks to millennia of overfishing, the Tyrrhenian Sea is rather impoverished. The most abundant species are small oily fish like anchovies and mackerel and cephalopods like squid and octopus. This octopus salad is inspired by Basilicata's short coastline, where octopi are fished from the sea, and the inland fields' waxy potatoes are plucked from the earth. Blanched green beans offer a bit of crunch and textural contrast.

Place the octopus, lemon zest, orange zest, peppercorns, bay leaf, rosemary, onion, and wine in a large pot. Cook over medium heat, allowing the octopus to cook in its own juices (after a minute or two, it will start to lose water). Cover and cook until the octopus is fork-tender, about 45 minutes. Remove the pot from the heat and allow the octopus to cool completely in its own juices, about 30 minutes. Cut into 1-inch segments.

Meanwhile, place the potatoes in a separate large pot and add enough cold water to cover. Salt the water (see page 31). Bring to a boil over medium-high heat and cook the potatoes until fork-tender, about 30 minutes. Drain and allow to cool slightly. Peel the potatoes and cut into 1-inch cubes.

While the octopus and potatoes are cooling, in a large bowl, whisk together the olive oil, lemon juice, mint, parsley, and pepper.

Add the potatoes to the bowl and toss with the vinaigrette while still warm, then add the octopus and olives.

Fill a medium bowl with ice and water. Fill the cleaned pot used to boil the potatoes with water and bring to a boil over high heat. Blanch the green beans in the boiling water for 1 minute, working in batches as needed. Drain the green beans and immediately plunge them into the ice water bath. Drain again.

Add the green beans to the bowl with the octopus. Toss well, season with salt and pepper, and add more olive oil as needed. (Warm potatoes can absorb a lot of oil, so you may need a bit more than suggested.) Serve immediately.

Come Pulire il Pesce

Cleaning Fish

Salted Anchovies

To clean salted anchovies, rinse them under cold running water and rub gently to loosen the salt and scales. With your fingers, break off the tail fin, then loosen and remove the spine. Rinse well and soak in cold water. After 15 minutes, taste an anchovy. If it is extremely salty, repeat this process until just slightly salty.

Whole Fish

In the fish markets of the south, fresh fish are sold whole in overflowing bins. Fishmongers will clean them upon request, but they are easy enough to do on your own. To clean fresh anchovies, pull off the head and the guts will follow. Most anchovies are small enough that their bones aren't super hard, so you can leave the spine in, if you wish, and eat the whole thing.

To clean sardines, mullets, and other whole fish, use a dull blade or the non-sharpened side of a paring knife to remove the scales, scraping the skin from the tail and working toward the head. Rinse under cold water. Beginning at the tail end, carefully slice open the belly of the fish. Use your fingers to remove the organs. Discard. Rinse the inside of the fish and pat dry with paper towels. There is no need to remove the head or bones.

Cuttlefish and Octopus

To clean a cuttlefish, separate the head and tentacles from the body; they will come away in one piece. Rinse the body under cold running water. Feel for the bone and tug it out, tearing through the outer skin that holds it in place. Peel off the skin under cold running water and discard. Discard the part of the head that contains the eyes, intestines, and hard beak.

To clean an octopus, separate the head from the body with a sharp knife just between the eyes and legs. Remove and discard the eyes and scrape out the entrails and ink sack from the head and discard as well.

Mussels

Inspect the mussels, discarding any that are open or broken. Rinse and scrub them under cold running water as needed to remove any debris and remove and discard the beard.

To open mussels to make *Cozze Ripiene* (page 119), gently but firmly press the shells together until a little opening forms on the edge where you can slide your knife in. You want the mussels to remain attached to their respective shells and for the shells to remain attached by their natural hinges.

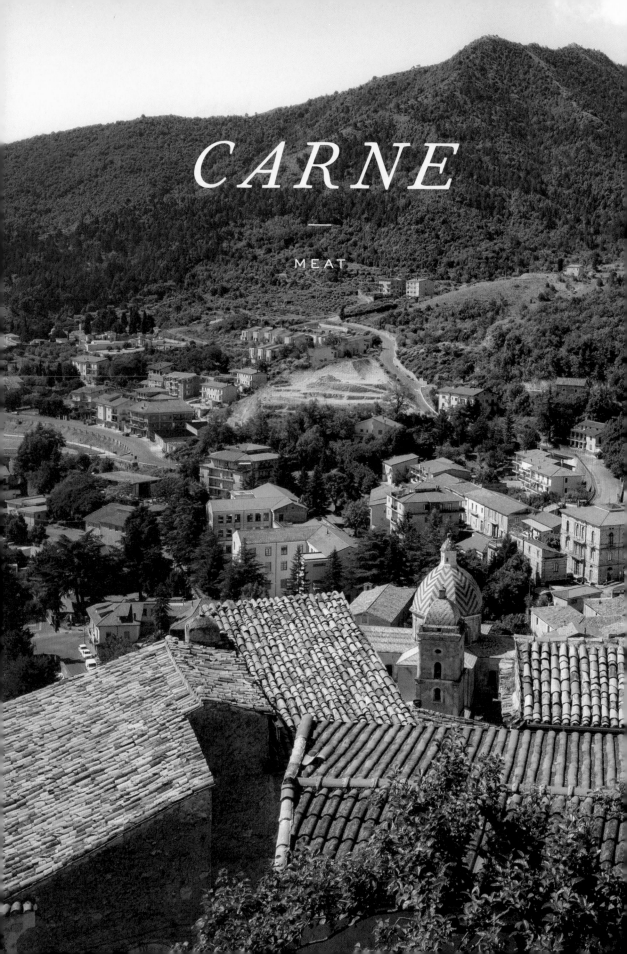

CARNE

—

MEAT

INVOLTINI ALLA PIAZZETTA

Frittata-Stuffed
Meat Rolls

Serves 4 to 6

4 eggs, beaten

½ cup finely grated Pecorino Romano

Handful of fresh mint, chopped

Sea salt and freshly ground black
     pepper

4 tablespoons extra-virgin olive oil

1 pound rump roast, cut into roughly
     3-ounce slices

1 garlic clove, smashed

1 (28-ounce) can whole tomatoes,
     crushed by hand

5 or 6 fresh basil leaves

1 cup dry white wine

NOTE The frittata is finished when it is neither wet nor wobbly and is cooked through without being dry or leathery. Flip the frittata by setting a small plate on top of the pan and using a gloved hand to carefully flip everything upside down, then slide the frittata, cooked-side up, right back into the hot pan.

In Cilento's Valle dell'Angelo, La Piazzetta, the only restaurant in town, exclusively serves hearty country dishes thoughtfully prepared by chef Carmela Bruno. In spite of Cilento being famous for its rugged coastline and pristine cerulean waters, most of this subregion of Campania is inland and populated with more grazing animals than people (the population of Valle dell'Angelo, for instance, is 156 and falling). Accordingly, the meat is culled from lean, free-range cows and, in this recipe, the herbs they graze on. Hold on to any leftover sauce and use it to dress pasta over the following days. I love it with ziti, rigatoni, or *carrati* (see page 92).

In a medium bowl, whisk together the eggs, Pecorino Romano, mint, salt, and pepper.

Heat 2 tablespoons of the olive oil in a small nonstick skillet over low heat. When the oil begins to shimmer, add the egg mixture to the skillet. Using a wooden spoon, stir a few times, moving from the outside of the pan toward the center. When the eggs are set in the middle, gently flip the frittata (see Note), cover, and cook until the edges start to come away from the sides of the pan and the middle starts to rise. Remove the pan from the heat and allow the frittata to cool before unmolding, about 20 minutes. To unmold, run a heatproof spatula around the edges and underneath the frittata and slide it onto a serving plate. Slice into 6 roughly equal pieces (long rectangles the width of the meat slices).

Lay the slices of beef flat on your work surface and season with salt and pepper on both sides. Place one piece of frittata at one short end of the meat. Roll the meat around the frittata, forming a medium-tight *involtino*. Use twine or a couple of toothpicks inserted flush with the meat to keep the roll closed. Repeat.

Heat the remaining 2 tablespoons olive oil in a large skillet over medium-high heat. When the oil begins to shimmer, add the *involtini* and brown them on all sides, about 5 minutes. Remove the rolls from the pan and set aside.

Reduce the heat to medium-low, add the garlic to the pan, and cook, stirring occasionally, until it just turns golden, about 5 minutes. Stir in the tomatoes and the basil. Season with salt. Bring to a simmer, then add the wine. When the sauce begins to simmer again, about 3 minutes, reduce the heat to low and return the *involtini* to the pan. The meat should be mostly covered by the tomato sauce. Cook, covered, until the meat is fork-tender, 1½ to 2 hours. Season with salt and pepper. Serve immediately, or allow the dish to rest in the refrigerator for up to 3 days to further develop the flavors.

SUSCIELLO

Eggs with Salami
and Tomato

Serves 4 to 6

---

1 tablespoon extra-virgin olive oil

2½ ounces pancetta, diced
(about ½ cup)

1 onion, roughly chopped

Sea salt

1 Italian sausage link, casing removed

2½ ounces *soppressata*, cut into ¼-inch
rounds (about ½ cup)

½ (14-ounce) can tomato sauce

6 eggs

Freshly ground black pepper

Many South Italy dishes fall into the category known as *piatti di ricupero,* which roughly translates to "dishes made from food scraps." Generally speaking, these *piatti* pack maximum caloric impact and use up leftovers, a necessity back when most Italians worked labor-intensive jobs in fields and needed all the nutrition they could get. *Susciello* combines ends of salami and other cured meats with eggs in what could be characterized as a tremendously tref *shakshuka.* Some cooks scramble their eggs, while others leave them whole. I have taken the latter approach, but feel free to improvise. I like to serve it over slices of toasted *Pane di Matera* (page 198).

Heat the olive oil in a large skillet over low heat. When the oil begins to shimmer, add the pancetta and cook until the fat has rendered, about 10 minutes. Add the onion and a pinch of salt and cook until soft and translucent, about 15 minutes. Add the sausage and *soppressata* and cook, stirring and breaking up the sausage with a wooden spoon, until the sausage is lightly browned, 5 to 7 minutes. Add the tomato sauce, season with salt, and simmer until the sauce has reduced slightly and lost its raw flavor, about 15 minutes. If the sauce seems too tight or dry, add hot water ¼ cup at a time to loosen.

One at a time, gently break the eggs into the sauce, spacing apart, cover, and cook, basting the eggs with the sauce, until whites have set but the yolks are still runny, about 6 minutes. Season with salt and pepper and serve immediately.

TRIPPA ALLA SCAPECE

Marinated Tripe
with Herbs

Serves 4 to 6

1½ pounds honeycomb tripe, washed

¼ cup sea salt, plus more as needed

3 tablespoons extra-virgin olive oil,
plus more for finishing

⅔ cup white wine vinegar

2 garlic cloves, thinly sliced

¼ cup fresh mint or basil leaves,
plus more for garnish

In the Parco del Pollino, cows graze on broad pastures dotted with countless varieties of wild mint. Most of these animals are destined to produce milk for caciocavallo, a semi-aged, pear-shaped cheese, but a few are raised for their meat and, by extension, their offal. At Luna Rossa in Terranova di Pollino, chef Federico Valicenti, a champion of local ingredients, simmers tripe, then marinates it with wild herbs and vinegar. The dish, *trippa alla scapece,* uses a phrase related to *escabeche,* a pickling method typical of Spanish cooking. You can substitute book tripe for the honeycomb tripe if you wish. Serve the *trippa* either on its own as a side dish or as a sandwich filling.

Place the tripe in a large pot and add enough cold water to cover. Bring to a boil over high heat. Drain and repeat. Drain again. Return the tripe to the pot and again add enough cold water to cover. Bring to a boil over medium-low heat. Add the salt and simmer until the tripe is fork-tender, about 3 hours. Drain, rinse under cold water, then cut the tripe into ½-inch strips.

In a large bowl, whisk together the olive oil, vinegar, garlic, and mint. Add the tripe strips and toss well to coat. Cover and marinate in the refrigerator for at least 2 hours or overnight.

Serve garnished with additional fresh mint and drizzled with olive oil.

CAPOCOLLO
AI FUNGHI

Pork Collar
with Mushrooms

Serves 12 to 15

1 (4-pound) boneless pork collar or butt, skin removed

2 tablespoons kosher salt

1 teaspoon freshly ground black pepper

2 tablespoons extra-virgin olive oil

2 garlic cloves, finely chopped

Leaves from 8 springs fresh thyme, finely chopped

1 teaspoon fennel pollen or ground fennel seeds

1 pound oyster mushrooms, sliced

¼ cup dry red wine (I like Aglianico del Vulture)

If you grew up Italian American, you're probably familiar with capocollo (called "gabagool" in my native New Jersey) in the form of cured deli meat served inside Italian hoagies. In Italy, we eat plenty of cured capocollo, too, but it often appears roasted, especially in the mountainous villages of Calabria's Parco Nazionale della Sila, where dozens of mushroom varieties grow in the region's thick forests. This recipe uses pork collar that has been marinated overnight, then cooked slowly to break down the muscle and fat until they are exquisitely tender. If you don't have a butcher who can provide the pork collar for you, feel free to substitute another fat-marbled cut like shoulder. This recipe admittedly makes a lot of pork, so either treat it as the centerpiece of a feast or plan to have leftovers, which make great sandwich fillings.

Place the pork collar in a flameproof roasting pan. In a small bowl, mix together the salt, pepper, olive oil, garlic, thyme, and fennel pollen. Using your hands, massage the marinade over the meat, distributing it evenly. Cover the pan with plastic wrap and refrigerate overnight.

The next day, preheat the oven to 200°F.

Redistribute the marinade over the meat evenly. Roast the pork collar until tender and the internal temperature reaches 125°F, about 2 hours. Remove from the oven and set aside to rest for 15 to 20 minutes.

Meanwhile, switch the oven to broil.

Return the pork collar to the oven and broil until evenly browned and the internal temperature reaches 140°F, 3 to 5 minutes, turning halfway through. Remove from the oven and set aside on a plate to rest for at least 20 minutes before slicing.

While the pork rests, set the roasting pan on the stovetop over medium heat. Add the mushrooms, working in batches as needed, and cook, stirring, until lightly browned, 4 to 5 minutes. Add the wine, stirring to scrape up any browned bits from the bottom of the pan, and cook until the liquid has reduced by half. Season the mushrooms with salt.

Serve the pork collar sliced with the mushrooms and sauce spooned over the meat.

L'Uccisione del Maiale
Pig Slaughter

Warning: The following feature discusses pig slaughter, which might be offensive to some readers.

Until the mid-twentieth century, the winter pig slaughter was, with the exception of the grape harvest, the only food ritual carried out on a large scale in every Italian region. Lots of rural families would raise pigs and slaughter them at home between late November and early February, when frigid temperatures could aid in the preservation of the meat, blood, and offal. In some places, the precise day was chosen based on the lunar cycle, while in others, families would wait until their pig reached a minimum weight or the temperature dropped to freezing. In the weeks preceding the slaughter, pigs would be fed a rich diet of potatoes, apples, kitchen scraps, whey from cheese making, and wheat bran from milling.

In the second half of the twentieth century, Italy became an increasingly urban nation; the number of small-scale farms declined, and so did the custom of home slaughter. In the early 1990s, laws were passed forbidding the custom, mandating that it take place at an officially sanctioned slaughterhouse. The recipes and rituals related to the millennial tradition of home pig slaughter have largely vanished as a result. On the big day, women would wake up before dawn to boil water to be used to remove the pig's tough bristles. Meanwhile, men awoke at dawn to sharpen knives. Before slaughter, the pig's snout would be bound and its body restrained and either laid out on a slab or strung up by its back feet. Then its neck would be sliced and its blood collected in a bucket below. The blood was among the first foods to be prepared; it would be heated in a double boiler with cocoa, sugar, walnuts, pine nuts, and orange zest to make a delicious dessert called *sanguinaccio*. In 1992 the EU banned the sale of and use in food of pig's blood, causing a seasonal specialty to virtually vanish from Italy; some cooks dedicated to their family traditions take the risk and illegally slaughter pigs at home or use contraband blood to make *sanguinaccio*.

The next steps were to boil off the bristles and remove the skin. The genitals were removed to be processed into grease for carpenter's saws. Then the head was removed, followed by the bladder. After being washed, the bladder might be filled with lard or roughly chopped seasoned meat. The other organs would be harvested and then the women would commence the long process of cleaning the intestines in water spiked with lemon and orange juice or vinegar. After a hearty breakfast of sautéed lungs and livers, the men would rest while the women continued sanitizing.

The meat would then be rubbed with salt and orange halves and set aside to rest until the following day, when it would be broken down for whole muscle cures, sausages, and lard. Until the 1950s, most peasants didn't do much mechanical grinding for their sausages and salamis, so everything was sliced by hand, salted, seasoned, and stuffed with fat into the intestine casings. Fresh sausages were for immediate consumption, while others would be hung to dry for aging.

Large muscle groups like capocollo (collar), pancetta (belly), *guanciale* (jowl), and prosciutto (haunch) would be salted and put away for months. Scraps would be cooked down to melt their fat for lard and *cicioli*, while the skin would be fashioned into gloves and shoes, the bristly hair into brushes, and the bones used to make glue or preserved in brine to use for future stock, one of the many ways the ritual of pig slaughter nourished South Italy throughout the year. Today these things, which were the norm for centuries, are precious novelties. Modernity might have its benefits, but traditions pay the price.

SPEZZATINO
ALL'UVA

Pork Cooked with Grapes

Serves 6 to 8

2 tablespoons extra-virgin olive oil

2 pounds boneless pork shoulder, salted (see page 32) and cut into 2-inch cubes

1 garlic clove, smashed

1 cup dry red wine (I like Aglianico del Vulture)

2 bay leaves

4 cups pork stock or water

1 bunch of red grapes (I like Tintilia grapes), halved and seeded

The foothills east of the Apennines in Molise grow Tintilia, an indigenous red grape known for its low yield and pleasant notes of red fruit and spices. Each year, the majority of the harvested grapes are pressed to make wine, with the remainder reserved for jams and even savory dishes like this pork and grape stew, which is made only at harvest time. The slight sweetness of the grapes mingles beautifully with the savory pork and herbaceous notes of the bay leaves. Salt the pork 24 hours in advance.

Heat the olive oil in a large skillet over medium heat. When the oil begins to shimmer, add the pork, working in batches as needed, and cook, turning, until it is browned on all sides, 7 to 8 minutes. Remove the pork and set aside on a plate.

Reduce the heat to low. Add the garlic and cook until just golden, about 5 minutes. Add the wine, increase the heat to medium, and scrape up any browned bits from the bottom of the pan. When the alcohol aroma dissipates and the liquid has nearly evaporated, about 2 minutes, add the bay leaves.

Return the pork to the pan. Add enough stock so the meat is mostly submerged and season with salt. Cook, stirring occasionally, for 1½ hours more, until the pork is fork-tender. Add the grapes at the 1¼ hour mark and continue cooking until they are tender. If the sauce becomes too dry, add a bit more stock (you may not need all the stock). Serve immediately.

CAPRETTO ARROSTITO

Country-Style Suckling Goat

Serves 6 to 8

1 bone-in goat shoulder
(about 4 pounds)

2 tablespoons kosher salt

2 teaspoons freshly ground black
pepper

2 tablespoons extra-virgin olive oil

2 garlic cloves, finely chopped

Leaves from 3 sprigs fresh rosemary,
finely chopped

6 fresh sage leaves, finely chopped

2 tablespoons white wine vinegar

1¼ cups dry white wine

¼ cup water

In the vertiginous terrain of the central Apennines, goats graze on chamomile, rosemary, and a vast buffet of wild herbs. This dish, a sort of hunter's-style roasted goat, would be at home on any country table in the spring, when kids are still suckling and their meat is tender and mild. Begin this recipe by marinating the goat overnight.

Place the goat shoulder in a flameproof roasting pan. In a small bowl, mix together the salt, pepper, olive oil, garlic, rosemary, and sage. Using your hands, massage the marinade over the meat, distributing it evenly. Cover the pan with plastic wrap and refrigerate overnight.

The next day, preheat the oven to 200°F.

Pour the vinegar over the meat and redistribute the marinade evenly. Roast the goat for 2 to 2½ hours, pouring 1 cup of the wine over the meat and turning it halfway through. The goat is done when it is golden brown and pulls away from the bone easily. Remove from the oven and set aside to rest for 15 to 20 minutes.

Meanwhile, switch the oven to broil.

Return the goat to the oven and broil until evenly browned, 3 to 5 minutes, turning it halfway through. Remove from the oven. Transfer the goat to a cutting board and allow to rest for at least 20 minutes before slicing.

Drain the goat drippings from the roasting pan into a clear container. Once the fat and juices separate, skim off the fat and discard. Set the pan on the stovetop over medium-low heat. When the pan is very hot, add the remaining ¼ cup wine and the water and scrape up any browned bits from the bottom of the pan. Add the degreseased pan juices and cook until the sauce has reduced by half, about 5 minutes.

Cut the goat into thick slices and serve with the pan sauce drizzled on top.

U' CUTTURIDD'

Lamb Stew

Serves 6 to 8

2 tablespoons extra-virgin olive oil

3½ pounds bone-in lamb shoulder or shank, salted in advance and cut into 2-inch pieces

1 garlic clove, smashed

1 onion, roughly chopped

Sea salt

1 *peperoncino* or 1 teaspoon red pepper flakes

3 bay leaves

1 cup dry white wine

½ (14-ounce) can whole tomatoes, crushed by hand

2 quarts *Brodo di Agnello* (lamb stock; recipe follows) or beef stock

Leaves from 6 sprigs fresh flat-leaf parsley, chopped

1 bunch wild fennel, chopped (optional)

Freshly ground black pepper

This Easter dish from the Murgia, the plateau straddling central Puglia and eastern Basilicata, is ancient shepherd food. The stew is called *cutturidd' d' pecura vecchia* in dialect in Basilicata, where it is made with mutton, and *u' cutturidd'* in Puglia, where it is made with suckling lamb. It was traditionally cooked in a *pignata*, a terra-cotta vessel that would be sealed with bread dough to steam the meat inside as it cooked, like a South Italian shepherd's pie. This is a simplified version cooked in a pot on the stovetop.

Heat the olive oil in a large pot over medium-high heat. When the oil begins to shimmer, add the lamb, working in batches as needed to prevent overcrowding, and sear for 3 to 4 minutes, until golden brown on all sides. Remove the lamb from the pot and set aside.

Reduce the heat to medium-low and add the garlic and onion. Season with salt and cook until the onion is soft and translucent, about 15 minutes. Add the *peperoncino* and bay leaves and cook until fragrant, about 1 minute. Add the wine and scrape up any browned bits from the bottom of the pan. When the alcohol aroma dissipates and the liquid has nearly evaporated, about 3 minutes, return the lamb to the pan. Add the tomatoes and enough stock so the meat is mostly submerged (you may not need all the stock). Season with salt. Cover the pot with the lid ajar and simmer until fork-tender but not quite falling off the bone, about 1½ hours. Add more warmed broth as needed to keep the lamb mostly submerged. Just before serving, stir in the parsley and wild fennel. Season with salt and black pepper. Serve at room temperature or reheated the next day.

Brodo di Agnello
Lamb Stock
Yields 4 quarts

A few lamb bones (ask your butcher to provide these), plus any trimmings from the lamb shoulder or shank

1 carrot, roughly chopped

1 onion, halved

1 celery stalk, roughly chopped

Put the lamb bones and trimmings in a large pot and add enough cold water to cover. Bring to a simmer over low heat, skimming off any scum that rises to the surface. Add the carrot, onion, and celery and simmer for at least 4 hours and up to 6 hours. Strain the stock, discarding the solids, and set aside until ready to use.

BRASATO DI BUFALA

Braised Buffalo

Serves 8 to 10

3½ pound chuck-eye or top blade roast of buffalo, bison, or veal, salted in advance and cut into 2-inch pieces

1 (750 milliliter) bottle dry red wine (I like Aglianico del Vulture)

3 bay leaves

1 tablespoon whole cloves

1 tablespoon finely chopped fresh rosemary

5 garlic cloves, smashed

2 tablespoons extra-virgin olive oil

3 ounces pancetta or *lardo* (cured fatback), diced (about ⅓ cup)

1 onion, diced

2 carrots, diced

2 celery stalks, diced

Sea salt

1 (14-ounce) can whole tomatoes, crushed by hand

2 cups beef stock

Freshly ground black pepper

NOTE For better searing, pat the marinated buffalo dry with paper towels before cooking in the rendered pancetta fat.

Most of Italy's buffalo are located in Campania, where they are used to produce milk for mozzarella (see page 42) and yogurt. Their dairy products (especially mozzarella) are transported all over Italy and beyond, while their meat rarely makes it out of the region and indeed is primarily consumed between Salerno and Cilento around Battipaglia, Paestum, and Capaccio. The most popular way it's prepared in the area is as a stew, marinating the lean meat in wine, then simmering to slowly tenderize it. If you can't get buffalo meat, substitute bison or veal. Whatever meat you choose, salt it in advance (see page 32).

Place the buffalo, wine, bay leaves, cloves, rosemary, and garlic in a large, nonreactive bowl. Cover with plastic wrap and refrigerate overnight or for up to 3 days, turning once a day. Remove the meat, reserving the marinade.

Heat the olive oil in a large pot over medium-low heat. When the oil begins to shimmer, add the pancetta. Cook until the fat renders, about 10 minutes. Remove the pancetta from the pot and set aside.

Increase the heat to medium, add the marinated buffalo, working in batches and turning as needed, and brown all over, about 10 minutes. Remove the buffalo from the pot and set aside.

Add the onion, carrots, and celery and season with salt. Cook, stirring, until the vegetables are softened, about 15 minutes. Return the pancetta to the pot. Add the reserved marinade, scraping up any browned bits from the bottom of the pan, and simmer until the liquid reduces by half, 10 to 15 minutes. Stir in the tomatoes and the stock and season with salt. When the sauce begins to simmer, return the buffalo to the pan. The meat should be mostly covered by the sauce. Cover and cook until fork-tender, 2 to 3 hours, checking occasionally to be sure the meat is at least two-thirds submerged and adding water as needed. Season with salt and pepper. Serve immediately or allow the dish to rest in the refrigerator for up to 3 days to further develop the flavors.

La Carne di Cavallo
Horsemeat

Italy imports more horsemeat—much of it from Eastern Europe—than any other country in the EU, and most of it is destined for Salento in Puglia and to southeastern Basilicata. Before industrialization, horsemeat was eaten out of pure necessity and was sourced locally. Peasants would slaughter their animals when they could no longer work and simmer their tough meat in tomato sauces to make dishes like *pezzetti di cavallu*, Salentine dialect for horse stew. Visit the trattorias of Salento, and you'll find this dish is still on many menus, although field horses have long since been replaced by tractors.

If you visit the area around the Puglia-Basilicata border, you'll find a number of dedicated horse butchers—look for signs in the window adverstising *carne equina* (horsemeat)—whose shops operate for retail orders during the day and as a restaurant counter at night. Places like Mimmo e Valeria in the village of Santeramo in Colle and Equineria da Mimmo in the town of Bernalda cut steaks to order for grilling over smoldering wood—just choose your preferred thickness and cooking temperature, just like you would for a beef steak. There are burgers, sausages, and meatballs, too, all made from horsemeat.

If you're based stateside, the idea of eating horse for pleasure rather than necessity will seem foreign; in the US, Congress recently lifted the ban on horse slaughter, but currently no slaughterhouses process horses. Meanwhile, in the Italian south, there's no stigma against eating horsemeat. Instead people embrace, rather than retreat from, their rural peasant origins, and in doing so preserve the flavors of the past.

POLLO *ALLA* POTENTINA

Potenza-Style Chicken
with Herbs and Wine

Serves 4 to 6

---

3 tablespoons pork lard or extra-virgin olive oil

1 whole chicken, salted in advance (see page 32) and cut into 8 pieces

1 onion, halved and cut into ¼-inch-thick slices, crosswise

2 garlic cloves, smashed

Sea salt

1 teaspoon *peperoncino* or red pepper flakes

½ cup dry white wine

4 ripe tomatoes, roughly chopped

5 or 6 fresh basil leaves

Potenza is the capital of Basilicata, the remote region of my maternal ancestry. A few years ago, when my mother and I visited the area to dig up some old family records, we made a detour through the city solely for the purpose of gazing at the Ponte Musmeci, a reinforced concrete bridge and supreme achievement of Brutalist architecture that crosses the Basento River at the edge of Potenza. Most visitors to Basilicata don't make it to this town—these days, they head to Matera or Bernalda, closer to the Puglia border—but we were glad we stuck around, and not just for the weird and wonderful bridge. Coincidentally, we encountered a procession for San Gerardo, Potenza's patron saint and, by extension, the chicken dish that locals make for this holiday. Chicken might not seem like a festive ingredient, but it was once quite a precious protein, and to this day, *potentini* celebrate with it. Salt the chicken 24 hours in advance.

Melt the lard in a large skillet over medium heat. When the fat shimmers, add the chicken, skin-side down, and cook, turning once, until browned on all sides, 8 to 10 minutes, adjusting the heat as needed to prevent burning. If the chicken skin sticks to the bottom of the pan while browning, do not force turning or flipping—it will release from the pan when it is ready. Remove the chicken from the pan and set aside.

Reduce the heat to low. Add the onion and garlic, season with salt, and cook until the onion is soft and translucent, about 15 minutes. Add the *peperoncino* and cook until fragrant, about 1 minute. Add the wine, increase the heat to medium, and scrape up any browned bits from the sides and bottom of the pan. When the alcohol aroma dissipates and the liquid has nearly evaporated, about 3 minutes, add the tomatoes and basil. Season with salt.

Return all the chicken pieces except the breasts to the pan and add enough water to cover it halfway. Cook, stirring occasionally, for 30 minutes, until the chicken is tender but not falling away from the bone and the sauce has reduced but is not dry. Return the chicken breasts to the pan. Cook on low until the internal temperature of the breast reaches 145°F, about 5 minutes more. If the sauce becomes too dry, add a bit more water. Serve immediately.

CONTORNI

—

SALADS AND SIDE DISHES

INSALATA DI RINFORZO

Cauliflower, Olive, Pepper, and Caper Salad

Serves 6

FOR THE QUICK-PICKLED VEGETABLES

3 cups white wine vinegar, plus more as needed

3 cups water

3 tablespoons kosher salt, plus more as needed

3 tablespoons sugar, plus more as needed

3 bay leaves

1 teaspoon whole black peppercorns

3 medium carrots, cut into ½-inch-thick rounds

2 red or yellow bell peppers, cut into 1-inch squares

2 celery stalks, cut into ½-inch-thick pieces

1 small red onion, halved and cut into ¼-inch-thick slices

FOR THE SALAD

Sea salt

1 small head cauliflower, separated into florets

½ cup olives, rinsed, pitted, and halved lengthwise

2 tablespoons capers, rinsed

6 salted anchovy fillets, cleaned (see page 134) and cut into ¼-inch pieces

¼ cup fresh flat-leaf parsley, roughly chopped

2 tablespoons white wine vinegar

¼ cup extra-virgin olive oil

Freshly ground black pepper

This Neapolitan holiday staple, also called *burdiglione*, is traditionally served on Christmas Eve to provide *rinforzo* (reinforcement) to a lean, fish-based meal. The ingredients are seasonal—Neapolitans pickle peppers after the summer harvest and begin using them once the weather cools. In Naples, the pepper of choice is the *pappacella*, a squat, flattened pepper, but you can substitute bell peppers or another sweet variety here. Some Neapolitan cooks also add torn escarole leaves to their *insalata*. Feel free to do so, but be sure to add them just before serving so they maintain their freshness and don't break down in the vinegar while the salad marinates overnight.

Make the quick-pickled vegetables: In a medium pot, combine the vinegar and water and bring to a simmer over low heat. Add the kosher salt and sugar. When both have dissolved, taste the brine; it should taste balanced, like something you would put on your salad. Adjust as needed, then add the bay leaves, peppercorns, carrots, and bell peppers. Return to a simmer and cook for 2 minutes, then add the celery. Return to a simmer and cook for 1 minute more, then add the onion and cook for 2 minutes more. Drain, transfer to a large bowl, and set aside to cool.

Make the salad: Fill a medium bowl with ice and water. Bring a medium pot of water to a boil over high heat. Salt the water (see page 31). When the salt has dissolved, add the cauliflower and cook until tender but still holding its shape, about 8 minutes. Drain and immediately plunge the cauliflower into the ice bath and let cool. Drain and transfer to the bowl with the pickled vegetables. Add the olives, capers, anchovies, and parsley. Pour the vinegar and olive oil over the vegetables and toss to coat. Season with sea salt and black pepper. Set aside in the refrigerator to allow the flavors to marry for at least 1 hour and up to 2 days before serving.

NOTE You can simmer each vegetable separately for more control over the final product. You want the vegetables to be al dente but cooked through. Cook the carrots and bell peppers for about 5 minutes each, the celery for about 3 minutes, and the onion for about 2 minutes.

Gli Ingredienti dal Mondo Arabo e dalle Americhe
Arab and New World Produce

The south's resources and position as a crossroads in the Mediterranean have made it a target for conquest and transit for millennia. As invaders and refugees made their way to the south, they brought their customs, cooking methods, and ingredients with them. At times, the locals would reject the new arrivals—both the people and their food—but after time had erased wounds, these foreigners and their imports would be adopted, wonderfully coloring the native traditions of the south with their influences.

One such event that shaped the south's produce in a way still appreciated today was the conquest of the south by Arabs in the ninth century AD. At this time, refined cane sugar arrived on the Italian peninsula and was ground into a paste with almonds—an ancient Greek import—to produce marzipan, or *pasta di mandorla*, as it's known in Puglia today. Eggplants, known to the Greeks and Romans, were reintroduced to South Italy by Arabs, and a huge range of eggplant species still flourish there. Most citrus fruits, with the exception of lemons, appear to have vanished from the peninsula after the fall of the Roman Empire, but bitter oranges returned to Italy once again to adorn the ornamental gardens of the Arab elite.

Sweet citrus did not arrive until the sixteenth century via the Spanish nobility, who ruled over South Italy until 1861. The Spanish are also responsible for introducing cotton and tobacco as cash crops following the discovery of the New World; Campania is still a major producer of the latter. The now ubiquitous prickly pear—and indeed every other cactus variety in Italy—was introduced by the Spanish as well.

American produce trickled into the heart of South Italy slowly. At first tomatoes and peppers, both members of the nightshade family, caused allergic reactions in the region's inhabitants, and it wasn't until centuries later that these New World foods were fully integrated into the diets of the south. Potatoes, one of the most important staples, and corn also arrived in the late fifteenth to early sixteenth centuries; both were immediately embraced by peasants as a valuable source of calories. Last but not least, the cocoa bean, another Spanish import from the New World, would be mashed with cane sugar to produce the first European chocolate bars almost five hundred years ago.

Across the south, from the most frenetic ports to the most isolated rural villages, ingredients from the Arab and New Worlds trickled in, eventually finding their place at the table.

CIANFOTTA

Serves 4 to 6

¼ cup extra-virgin olive oil

2 medium onions, diced

2 garlic cloves, smashed

2 potatoes, peeled and cut into
   1-inch cubes

2 bell peppers, cut into 1-inch squares

2 eggplants, cut into 1-inch cubes

3 tomatoes, chopped

3 young zucchini, cut into
   ½-inch-thick rounds

Sea salt

¼ cup fresh basil leaves, torn

Some Neapolitans say this dish is simplified French ratatouille, while others contend that ratatouille is complicated *cianfotta*. Either way, this stew is a tender medley of seasonal summer produce. While cooking *cianfotta*, as it's known in the local dialect (*ciambotta* in Italian), you want everything to sort of steam in its own juices; you'll need to control the heat so you don't need to add any water. In the end, the vegetables should be very soft and almost falling apart and the flavors should all be beautifully married.

Heat the olive oil in a large saucepan or deep skillet over medium-low heat. When the oil begins to shimmer, add the onions and garlic and season with salt. Cook until the onions are soft and translucent, about 15 minutes. Add the potatoes and cook for about 10 minutes more, then add the bell peppers and eggplants and cook for 10 minutes more. Add the tomatoes and zucchini, season with salt, and bring to a simmer.

Reduce the heat to low, cover, and simmer until the vegetables are all very soft and nearly falling apart, about 30 minutes. Add a bit of water to prevent sticking as needed.

Remove from the heat, stir in the basil, and serve warm or cooled. *Cianfotta* improves overnight and will keep in the refrigerator for up to 3 days.

PATATE RAGANATE

Crispy Potatoes with Onions and Parmigiano-Reggiano

Serves 4 to 6

---

3 large potatoes (I like Yukon Gold), peeled and cut into ¼-inch-thick slices

3 Tropea onions, halved and cut into ¼-inch-thick slices

1 large tomato, chopped

¼ cup plus 3 tablespoons extra-virgin olive oil

Sea salt

1 teaspoon dried oregano

½ cup finely grated Parmigiano-Reggiano

½ cup dried bread crumbs

Freshly ground black pepper

½ cup water

Tomatoes and eggplants might get all the attention in South Italy's markets and dishes, but potatoes are the true anchor of the south's myriad regional cuisines. From coast to coast and on the mountainous peaks in between, potatoes appear in soups, alongside meat, as side dishes, and even in desserts like *'Mpigne* (page 221). *Patate raganate* is just one of many side dishes from Basilicata where high-altitude potatoes are the protagonist. Don't be afraid to burn the edges a little; the crispy bits that stick to the pan are delicious.

Preheat the oven to 350°F.

In a large bowl, combine the potatoes, onions, tomato, and ¼ cup of the olive oil. Season with salt.

In a small bowl, combine the oregano, Parmigiano-Reggiano, bread crumbs, pepper, and 2 tablespoons of the olive oil. Mix with your hands until the mixture resembles moist sand.

Grease a baking dish with the remaining 1 tablespoon olive oil. Add the potato mixture, drizzle over the water, then sprinkle the bread crumb mixture evenly over the potatoes. Bake, uncovered, until the potatoes have a golden crust and the bread crumbs are well toasted, 1 to 1¼ hours. Serve immediately.

SEDANO ALLA MOLISANA

Sautéed Celery with Olives

Serves 4

Sea salt

1 bunch celery, sliced into 1-inch pieces (see Note)

5 tablespoons extra-virgin olive oil

6 spring onions or scallions, thinly sliced

½ cup Gaeta olives, rinsed, pitted, and cut in half lengthwise

Freshly ground black pepper

¼ cup *Pane Grattugiato* (seasoned bread crumbs; see page 121)

This humble side dish is the epitome of Molise's culinary simplicity. As with many dishes from the region, *sedano alla molisana* is enriched with bread crumbs to add a bit more flavor—and calories—to the peasant cuisine.

Preheat the oven to 400°F.

Bring a medium pot of water to a boil over high heat. Salt the water (see page 31). When the salt has dissolved, add the celery. Blanch for 1 minute, then drain and set aside.

Meanwhile, heat 3 tablespoons of the olive oil in a large skillet over medium-low heat. When the oil begins to shimmer, add the spring onions, season with salt, and cook until softened but not browned, about 3 minutes. Add the blanched celery and cook until tender, 15 minutes more. Add the olives and cook for 1 minute more. Season with salt and pepper.

Place the celery mixture in a small baking dish. Sprinkle the *Pane Grattugiato* on top and drizzle the remaining 2 tablespoons olive oil over the bread crumbs. Bake for 35 to 40 minutes, until the bread crumbs are lightly browned. The celery should be close to falling apart but still hold its form. Serve immediately.

NOTE The tougher outer stalks of the celery need to be cleared of strings, or else you'll end up with a few unpleasantly stringy mouthfuls. Using a vegetable peeler or small knife, remove most of the fiber from around the outside of the thickest stalks, then slice the stalks into 1-inch pieces.

CIAUDEDDA

Favas, Artichokes,
and Potatoes

Serves 4 to 6

1 tablespoon extra-virgin olive oil

½ cup diced pancetta

1 onion, diced

1 garlic clove, smashed

Sea salt

3 tender young artichokes, cleaned
and quartered

2 potatoes, peeled and cut into
1-inch cubes

Handful of chopped fresh herbs (such
as marjoram, thyme, mint, parsley)

Freshly ground black pepper

½ cup white wine

4 cups vegetable broth or water,
warmed

10 ounces shelled fresh fava beans

What *Cianfotta* (page 161) is to summer in Campania, *Ciaudedda* is to spring in Basilicata. This springtime stew is made in that narrow period in which artichokes and favas are both in season and the young favas are sweet and tender. It's not quite brothy, having absorbed most of the liquid during the simmering process, but it's not dry, either. It can be a side dish or even a main, and in fact it's quite popular as a *secondo* around Lent (minus the pancetta, of course).

Heat the olive oil in a large skillet over low heat. When the oil begins to shimmer, add the pancetta. Cook until the pancetta fat has rendered, about 10 minutes, then add the onion and garlic and season with salt. Cook until the garlic just begins to turn golden, about 5 minutes, then add the artichokes, potatoes, herbs, and pepper. Season once again with salt and stir to combine the ingredients.

Increase the heat to high and add the wine. Bring to a boil and cook until the alcohol aroma dissipates, 2 to 3 minutes, then add enough broth to cover the artichokes halfway. Return to a boil, reduce the heat to medium-low, and cook until the artichokes and potatoes begin to soften, 10 to 12 minutes. Add the favas, cover, and cook until the favas are soft and most of the liquid has been absorbed, about 20 minutes. If it looks like it's drying out too much, add more broth as needed (you may not need all the broth). Season with salt and pepper. Serve warm or at room temperature.

NOTE In South Italy, there are two diametrically opposed schools of thought when it comes to wine and artichokes. Some cooks are vehemently opposed to ever letting the two meet, citing the metallic flavor that results from drinking wine with artichokes. Others never pause for a second to consider it. I fall somewhere in the middle, but if you are in the former category, feel free to omit the wine from this recipe.

La Raccolta
Grape Harvest

Vineyards require maintenance throughout the year, from early spring when the first tendrils awaken following their winter slumber, until after the harvest in early fall when the vines are trimmed and manicured. Recipes related to each stage of vineyard upkeep were developed by poor families working in these fields. Their need for energy knew no bounds during the course of this taxing labor, so not only would they drink wine before and after work as a calorie source, but they would even eat the trimmed tendrils, vines, and leaves.

Now that much of the south's wine industry has gone mechanized—and therefore vineyard workers aren't quite as numerous or as hungry as they used to be—many of these old-school recipes have virtually vanished. That includes *insalata di viticci,* a salad made with the green shoots that appear on vines in early spring. They are trimmed from the plant, simmered in vinegar, and dressed with olive oil and herbs. Unless you go foraging for them yourself and make it at home, one of the few places you'll find this disappearing dish is in Puglia in the village of Noci, where it is served in the spring at L'Antica Locanda as part of the trattoria's famously abundant *antipasto* spread.

'U PAN' CUOTT'

Baked Bread and
Provolone Casserole

Serves 4 to 6

1 pound day-old durum wheat bread
(I like Matera-style; see page 198),
torn into bite-size pieces

3 cups cherry tomatoes, halved

7 ounces provolone cheese, cut into
1-inch cubes

1 teaspoon *peperoni cruschi* powder or
sweet paprika

2 garlic cloves, smashed

1 teaspoon dried oregano

½ teaspoon *peperoncino* or red pepper
flakes

¼ cup plus 2 tablespoons extra-virgin
olive oil

Sea salt

In Bernalda, a town in Basilicata best known as the ancestral village of Francis Ford Coppola, there are many ancient bread traditions. The town isn't far from the durum wheat fields of the Murgia plateau and the famous bread towns Matera and Altamura. One of the town's classic dishes is *'u pan' cuott'* (Bernaldese dialect for *pane cotto*, "cooked bread"). Families would bake stale slices of Bernalda's enormous 3-kilogram loaves with whatever food scraps they could find, resulting in a savory, delicious bread casserole bound by gooey bits of melted provolone. Use the crustiest durum bread you can find or bake.

Preheat the oven to 475°F with a rack in the center position.

Place the bread in a colander, rinse with warm water, and set aside to soften. The bread should be moistened but not sopping wet.

In a large bowl, combine the tomatoes, provolone, *peperoni cruschi*, garlic, oregano, *peperoncino,* and ¼ cup of the olive oil. Season with salt.

When the bread crusts have softened, squeeze out any excess liquid and add the bread to the bowl with the tomato mixture. Stir to combine.

Grease a baking dish with 1 tablespoon of the olive oil, pour in the tomato mixture, and drizzle the remaining 1 tablespoon olive oil on top. Bake until the top is heavily browned and the provolone has melted, about 20 minutes. Serve warm.

The concept that vast criminal organizations still exist and influence Italian society might seem quaint or anachronistic. Maybe that's because so much of what outsiders think they know about the Mafia is informed by *The Godfather*, a film that's nearly fifty years old. Certainly, if reporting on the Mafia wasn't a life-threatening occupation, we would all know a lot more. Indeed, it's not unusual for several dozen journalists at a given time to be under 24-hour police protection for reporting on the topic.

What *has* been documented by some brave journalists and human rights groups is that the Camorra and the 'Ndrangheta, the Mafias of Campania and Calabria, respectively, are deeply entrenched in the food systems of the south. They prey on vulnerable migrants—men, women, and children, mainly from Central Africa and South Asia, trafficked into Italy by other Mafias—and force them into modern-day slavery. There are an estimated 130,000 migrant workers harvesting produce in the fileds of the Italian south, for whom working twelve to fourteen hours a day, six or seven days a week, often nets less than 150 euro, well short of Italy's 9 euro per hour minimum wage. From that sum, field bosses often charge extortionate prices for transportation, food, and water. And violence against and intimidation of these agricultural workers is rampant.

Italy's homegrown crime groups have plenty to gain from these cruel, exploitative practices. Mafia influence pervades the food and farming

sectors, deriving both illegal and legitimate profits from their agriculture businesses. The corruption is so extensive, it's nearly impossible to ensure that the food we eat, whether it's citrus from Calabria, tomatoes from Campania, or artichokes from Puglia, has been harvested by people earning a dignified, living wage, or any wage at all, unless you go directly to the source. Fortunately, Gustiamo, a Bronx-based purveyor of Italian foods, does just that. By purchasing products from farms that have been inspected by Gustiamo's founder, Beatrice Ughi, and her staff, you can fight the Mafia from the safety of your own home with every online purchase.

FINOCCHI IN PADELLA

Sautéed Fennel and Herbs

Serves 4 to 6

3 fennel bulbs

¼ cup extra-virgin olive oil

2 garlic cloves, smashed

1 teaspoon fresh thyme

½ cup water

Sea salt

⅓ cup finely grated Parmigiano-Reggiano

¼ cup *Pane Grattugiato* (seasoned bread crumbs; see page 121)

Freshly ground black pepper

This side dish from Molise, like many of the region's *cucina povera*, or peasant cuisine, features bread crumbs stirred in to provide an extra caloric boost to a lean diet. Today, the economic realities and nutritional necessities of *molisani* have changed, so you can feel free to exclude the dried bread crumbs called for in the recipe, as they change the texture and make the dish a bit sticky and clumpy. The fennel here is accompanied by garlic, thyme, Parmigiano-Reggiano, and black pepper, which mingle with and mellow out the fennel's natural sweetness.

Trim and discard the stalks and root ends from the fennel bulbs, reserving the fronds. Roughly chop the fronds and set aside. Remove any tough outer layers or peel the outer layer with a vegetable peeler to remove any tough fibers. Slice the bulbs in half through the root end and then slice each half lengthwise into ¼-inch-thick pieces. Set aside.

Heat the olive oil in a large skillet over medium-low heat. When the oil begins to shimmer, add the garlic and cook until it just begins to turn golden, about 5 minutes. Add the thyme and cook until fragrant, 30 seconds more.

Add the fennel and water and season with salt. Increase the heat to medium, cover, and cook until the fennel is very tender, 15 to 20 minutes. Uncover, add the fennel fronds, and cook until any remaining water has evaporated, about 5 minutes more. The fennel should be nearly falling apart. Remove the skillet from the heat and stir in the Parmigiano-Reggiano and *Pane Grattugiato*. Season with salt and pepper and serve warm.

INSALATA DI LIMONE

Lemon and Mint Salad

Serves 6 to 8

6 untreated organic lemons (I like Meyer lemons), seeded and cut into bite-size pieces

Handful of fresh mint leaves, torn

1 teaspoon *peperoncino* or red pepper flakes

3 tablespoons extra-virgin olive oil

Sea salt

At Da Girone, a raucous seaside restaurant in Procida, this salad is served as a foil for the establishment's numerous fried fish dishes. I love it after a long day of sunning myself on Procida's "Il Postino" beach, named for its role as a backdrop in the Academy Award–winning film of the same name. Just as any Procidan would, use the best-quality lemons you can find—and don't peel them! The contrast of the flesh, pith, and skin give this salad surprising depth.

In a medium bowl, combine the lemons, half the mint, the *peperoncino*, and the olive oil. Season with salt and toss well. Set aside to marinate for at least 1 hour. Serve garnished with the remaining mint.

NOTE A lot of this dish is about making a strongly flavored citrus fruit subtler, which is achieved, in part, by making thin slices: Halve the lemons. Slice each half into thirds lengthwise, then crosswise into ⅛-inch-thick slices—or thinner, if you can!

INSALATA DI PERA, RUGHETTA, E SCAMORZA

Pear, Arugula, and
Scamorza Salad

*Serves 4 to 6 as a side dish or
appetizer, or 3 or 4 as a main dish*

3 tablespoons extra-virgin olive oil,
plus more for greasing

1 pound *scamorza* cheese, cut into
½-inch-thick rounds

1 small, firm pear (I like Bartlett),
cored and cut into ⅛-inch-thick
slices

12 ounces arugula

1½ tablespoons fresh lemon juice

Sea salt and freshly ground black
pepper

At La Grotta di Zi' Concetta in Campobasso, the rustic dishes are simple and rarely exceed three ingredients. This one, which can be a main or a side dish, features grilled *scamorza* cheese with peppery wild arugula and sweet local pears. *Scamorza* is mozzarella's cousin; it's a salted cow's-milk cheese made from stretched curds that are shaped into a spherical form, then wrapped with twine and hung up to age, resulting in a pear-shaped cheese—it's only a coincidence that its flavor goes so well with pears!

Lightly grease a grill pan or skillet and heat the pan over high heat. Grill the *scamorza* until crisp on the outside and soft and slightly melted inside, about 2 to 3 minutes per side. Set aside while dressing the salad.

In a large bowl, combine the pear, arugula, olive oil, and lemon juice. Season with salt and pepper. Toss with your hands.

Serve the *scamorza* alongside the pear salad.

PANE, FOCACCIA, E PIZZA

—

BREAD, FOCACCIA, AND PIZZA

FOCACCIA PUGLIESE

Olive and Tomato Flatbread

Makes three 10- to 12-inch focaccie

---

350 grams (1½ cups) filtered water

200 grams (1⅔ cups) bread flour, plus more for dusting

300 grams (1¾ cups) *farina di semola rimacinata* (fancy durum flour; see page 203)

100 grams (3½ ounces) riced boiled potato, cooled

2 grams (½ rounded teaspoon plus a pinch) active dry yeast

12 grams (2 teaspoons) sea salt, plus more as needed

5 grams (1 rounded teaspoon) sugar

155 grams (¾ cup) extra-virgin olive oil, plus more for greasing

500 grams (1 pound) mature cherry tomatoes

About 30 black olives

3 grams (1 tablespoon) dried oregano

NOTE To get the unique texture of *Focaccia Pugliese*, you need to bake with intense heat from underneath. Since these conditions are difficult to replicate in a home oven, you will get the best results by using a frying pan or skillet with only metal and no plastic or wood parts for baking the *focaccie*. If you have enough all-metal 10- to 12-inch-diameter pans for all three *focaccie*, you can prepare them simultaneously. Otherwise, bake one and store the others in the refrigerator until you are ready to bake them to prevent them from overfermenting at room temperature.

Just as Naples is the capital of Italy's thick-rimmed wood-fired pizza pies, Bari and its surrounding towns are home to a beloved regional flatbread, *Focaccia Pugliese*. This rich, high-hydration dough is baked in seasoned sheet pans at places like Panificio Fiore on Strada Palazzo di Città in Bari Vecchia. The pan is drenched in oil before the dough is stretched into place, so when it all goes into the oven, the dough practically fries as it bakes, rendering the bottom crispy and pleasantly charred. This recipe features cherry tomatoes and olives, but you can use onions or even blind-bake the dough, omitting the toppings and just seasoning with salt and herbs.

In the bowl of a stand mixer fitted with the dough hook, combine the water, bread flour, *farina di semola rimacinata,* riced potato, yeast, salt, sugar, and 50 grams (¼ cup) of the olive oil. Mix on low for 2 minutes, then increase the speed to medium and mix for 18 minutes more. The dough will come together and become smooth and slightly sticky.

Turn the dough out onto a lightly floured surface, allowing it to gently release from the bowl, and cut it into 3 equal pieces, weighing about 330 grams (11½ ounces) each, with a dough scraper or knife. Shape each piece into a ball and place each separately on a deep plate generously greased with olive oil. Brush lightly with olive oil and cover with plastic wrap. Set aside to rise at room temperature for 2 hours, until almost tripled in size.

Pour 25 grams (2 tablespoons) of the olive oil into a 10- to 12-inch pan (see Note), tilting the pan to coat the entire bottom and 1 inch up on the sides. Turn one of the dough balls out into the pan. Using greased fingertips, carefully push and stretch the dough into the shape of the pan, taking care not to tear it.

Gently press a third of the halved cherry tomatoes, cut-side down, and about 10 olives into the dough, distributing them evenly. Cover the pan with a clean kitchen towel and set aside to rise at room temperature for 20 minutes.

Meanwhile, preheat the oven to 425°F with the rack in the center position.

Remove the towel and sprinkle about 1 teaspoon of the oregano over the dough. Season with salt. Drizzle 10 grams olive oil over the dough, distributing it evenly.

(recipe continues)

Using greased fingertips, press into the dough around the tomatoes and olives to form dimples.

Place the pan over medium-high heat. When the oil starts to bubble and crackle, cook for 3 minutes more. Check the underside of the dough by gently lifting it with a heatproof spatula. It should be a very dark golden color. If it has not browned, cook for 30 seconds to 1 minute more.

Transfer the pan to the oven and bake until the *focaccia* has a dark golden crispy crust, about 17 minutes; *focaccie* brown irregularly, so having darker spots mixed with lighter parts is normal. Transfer the *focaccia* to a wire rack and allow to cool for 5 minutes before slicing.

Repeat with the remaining dough, cooling the pan and allowing the oven to return to the desired temperature before baking the next *focaccia*.

PUCCE ULIATE

Olive Rolls

Makes 8 pucce

325 grams (2 cups) *farina di semola rimacinata* (fancy durum flour; see page 203), plus more for dusting

175 grams (1 cup plus 2 tablespoons) bread flour

2½ grams (scant 1 teaspoon) active dry yeast

9 grams (1½ teaspoons) sea salt

10 grams (2 teaspoons) honey

30 grams (2 tablespoons) extra-virgin olive oil, plus more for greasing

370 grams (1½ cups) filtered water

120 grams (¾ cup) Gaeta olives, pitted and halved lengthwise

Salento, the extreme southern tip of Puglia's long and varied region, is home to some of Italy's most ancient olive trees. Some bear fruit for oil, while others grow olives for brining. They appear whole (pit in—watch out!) in breads throughout the region, including in *pucce*, Salento's typical bread. These small durum wheat olive rolls have been modified from the Salentine recipe to exclude the pits!

In the bowl of a stand mixer fitted with the dough hook, combine the *farina di semola rimacinata*, bread flour, yeast, salt, honey, olive oil, and 250 grams (1 cup) of the water. Mix on low speed until there is no more dry flour in the bowl, about 3 minutes. Cover the bowl with plastic wrap and allow to rest for 20 minutes. Return the bowl to the mixer, then mix on medium and add the remaining water a little bit at a time over the course of 3 to 4 minutes. When all the water has been incorporated, increase the speed to medium-high and mix for 8 minutes more, until the dough is smooth and elastic. Reduce the speed to low, add the olives, and mix until incorporated.

Place the dough in a medium bowl greased with olive oil. With one hand, lightly grasp one edge of the dough. Pull this flap of dough upward and outward, then attach it to the top of the dough. Turn the bowl a 45 degree turn and repeat until you have rotated the bowl a complete turn. Flip the dough over, cover the bowl with plastic wrap, and place in the refrigerator to rise at 39°F to 41°F for 12 hours.

Meanwhile, cover a clean, dry work surface with a thick layer of durum flour. Line a baking sheet with parchment paper. Wet your hands and pinch off pieces of about 125 grams (4½ ounces) each. Pass the pieces through the durum flour and transfer to the prepared baking sheet, spacing at least 2 inches apart. Using the palm of your hand, press down on the dough to flatten. Cover the whole baking sheet with plastic wrap and allow to rise at room temperature for 1 hour.

Preheat the oven to 475°F with a rack in the center position.

Remove the plastic wrap from the dough and spray the *pucce* with water. Bake for 5 minutes, then reduce the oven temperature to 410°F. Bake until the *pucce* take on a golden color and sound hollow when tapped on the bottom, about 15 minutes more.

Transfer to a wire rack and allow to cool to room temperature.

CASATIELLO

Easter Bread

Serves 12

South Italy's tables are renowned for their decadent holiday meals, but nothing quite rivals the multi-day feast of Easter. Especially after the ascetic Lenten period, devout Catholics are eager to break their fast and commemorate the resurrection with symbolic foods. For South-dwellers and especially Neapolitans, *Casatiello* is the iconic savory bread for this holiday time. The best versions feature lard from recently slaughtered pigs (see page 144) and inlaid eggs symbolizing the Resurrection.

FOR THE DOUGH

600 grams (4¾ cups) bread flour

2 grams (1 teaspoon) active dry yeast

10 grams (2 teaspoons) sea salt

1 gram (2 large pinches) freshly ground black pepper

50 grams (¼ cup) lard, plus more for greasing

300 grams (1¼ cups plus 2 tablespoons) filtered water

FOR THE FILLING

60 grams (2 ounces) lard, at room temperature, plus more for the pan

2 grams (heaping 1 teaspoon) freshly ground black pepper

75 grams (2½ ounces) finely grated Pecorino Romano or Parmigiano-Reggiano

150 grams (5 ounces) salami, cut into ½-inch cubes

150 grams (5 ounces) cooked ham or mortadella, cut into ½-inch cubes

150 grams (5 ounces) provolone or emmenthal cheese, cut into ½-inch cubes

60 grams (2 ounces) semi-aged pecorino, cut into ½-inch cubes

60 grams (2 ounces) cured pancetta, cut into ½-inch squares, ⅛ inch thick

60 grams (2 ounces) prosciutto, cut into ½-inch squares, ⅛ inch thick

4 hard-boiled eggs (optional)

1 egg, beaten

Make the dough: In the bowl of a stand mixer fitted with the dough hook, combine the flour, yeast, salt, pepper, lard, and filtered water. Mix on low until the dough starts to come together and there is no more dry flour in the bowl, about 2 minutes. Increase the speed to medium and mix until smooth, elastic, and soft, but not sticky, about 10 minutes.

Turn the dough out onto a work surface, shape into a tight ball, and return to the bowl of the stand mixer. Cover the bowl with plastic wrap and allow the dough to rest at room temperature until it has almost tripled in size, about 3 hours.

When the dough has risen, make the filling: If you are going to bake eggs into the top of the *casatiello*, cut away about 60 grams (2 ounces) of the dough and set it aside to use as "egg cages." Roll out the remaining dough into a rectangle that measures approximately 12 × 20 inches. (This can be done on an unfloured surface thanks to the fat content of the dough, which will keep it from sticking.) Using a spatula, spread the lard over the dough. Sprinkle the pepper and Pecorino Romano over the lard. Distribute the salami, ham, provolone, semi-aged pecorino, pancetta, and prosciutto over the dough, pressing lightly and leaving a 1-inch border along the edge of the long side of the dough farthest from you.

Starting from the long side closest to you, roll up the dough as tightly as possible without tearing it so you have a 20-inch-long roll. Seal the roll by pinching the seam along its entire length, then pinching closed the open ends, stuffing in any rogue bits of cheese or salami before sealing.

(recipe continues)

Grease a Bundt pan. Fit the roll snugly inside, connecting the ends by pinching them together. Place the 4 hard-boiled eggs (if using) on top of the dough, spacing them an equal distance apart. Gently press them into the dough. Roll the reserved dough into 8 equal strands and fasten them around each egg in the sign of a cross. Press the ends into the top of the casatiello. Cover with a kitchen towel and set aside to rise at room temperature for 1 hour.

Preheat the oven to 350°F.

Brush the egg over the dough and bake until the casatiello starts to brown, about 1 hour. If it darkens too quickly, cover with aluminum foil for the remaining baking time.

Remove the *casatiello* from the oven and set aside to cool for 1 hour before unmolding. Unmold and allow the *casatiello* to rest on a wire rack for 2 hours and up to 18 hours before slicing.

Serve at room temperature or lightly toasted.

PIZZA CHIENA

Egg and Ham Pie

Serves 12 to 15

Dialect for "stuffed pizza," the name *pizza chiena* barely does justice to this very decadent savory tart, which is packed with a potpourri of hams and cheeses all stuffed into an unctuous, flaky crust.

Make the dough: In the bowl of a stand mixer fitted with the dough hook, combine the flour, yeast, sugar, salt, egg, and water. Mix on low until the dough comes together and there is no more dry flour in the bowl, about 2 minutes. Increase the speed to medium and mix, adding the lard a little at a time, until the dough is smooth, elastic, and soft, but not sticky, about 10 minutes.

Turn the dough onto a floured work surface, shape it into a tight ball, and return it to the bowl of the stand mixer. Cover the bowl with plastic wrap and allow the dough to rest at room temperature for 2½ hours, or until it has at least doubled in size.

Meanwhile, make the filling: In a large bowl using a handheld mixer, beat together 10 of the eggs and the ricotta until smooth, about 1 minute. Add the *primo sale*, provolone, mozzarella, pecorino, Parmigiano-Reggiano, salami, ham, prosciutto, and pepper and stir.

Preheat the oven to 350°F with the rack in the center position. Lightly grease a 9-inch springform pan. Line a baking sheet with parchment.

Assemble the pizza: Divide the dough into two unequal pieces, about two thirds and one third. Roll out the larger piece of dough on a well-floured work surface to a diameter of at least 16 inches. Transfer it to the prepared springform pan, gently pressing it into the corners and up the sides, repairing any holes. The dough should overhang the sides of the pan. Roll out the smaller piece of the dough, then use a knife or pastry wheel to cut it to the exact diameter of the pan.

Pour the egg mixture into the dough-lined pan. Cover with the second piece of dough. Beat the remaining egg and brush some of it along the edges of the dough cover. Fold the overhanging dough over the egg-moistened dough lid and press to attach. Brush the dough all over with egg. Make a small hole in the center of the dough to allow steam to escape.

Place the pan on the prepared baking sheet. Bake until the filling is set and the crust is golden brown, about 1¼ hours. If the dough takes on too much color, cover with aluminum foil for the remaining baking time. Remove from the oven and set aside for at least 30 minutes before releasing from the springform pan. Allow to rest at room temperature for at least 12 hours before slicing.

FOR THE DOUGH

500 grams (4 cups) all-purpose flour, plus more for dusting

2¾ grams (1 rounded teaspoon) active dry yeast

Pinch of sugar

11 grams (2 rounded teaspoons) sea salt

1 egg

200 grams (¾ cup plus 2 teaspoons) filtered water

80 grams (3 ounces) lard, at room temperature, plus more for greasing

FOR THE FILLING

11 medium eggs

250 grams (9 ounces) ricotta (I like sheep's-milk ricotta)

150 grams (5 ounces) *primo sale* cheese or *queso blanco,* cut into ½-inch cubes

150 grams (5 ounces) provolone or *scamorza* cheese, cut into ½-inch cubes

125 grams (4½ ounces) mozzarella, cut into ½-inch cubes

60 grams (2 ounces) sharp pecorino or cheddar, cut into ½-inch cubes

60 grams (2 ounces) finely grated Parmigiano-Reggiano

120 grams (4 ounces) salami, cut into ⅓-inch cubes

200 grams (7 ounces) sliced ham, cut into 2-inch squares

150 grams (5 ounces) sliced prosciutto, cut into 2-inch squares

2 grams (1 heaping teaspoon) freshly ground black pepper

Kneading Dough

All the doughs in this chapter can be mixed by hand
with some small changes. Hand-kneading takes a bit
more time, so simply add a few minutes to the time
suggested for mixing with a stand mixer.

Mixing and kneading by hand puts you in direct
contact with the dough and forges a bond between you
and the final product. It will also give you a greater
understanding of how flour and water react, what
happens to the dough as it ferments, how strong it is,
and when it is perfectly risen. No matter how tacky the
dough is, it will develop and tighten up naturally as the
gluten develops. When you have mastered the basics—
including how the dough interacts with the humidity of
your climate and kitchen—you can start to play with
small changes to the recipe.

If intense kneading isn't your thing, you can add
a few 15- to 20-minute resting periods between rounds
of kneading. If you do add extra resting periods, just be
sure to delay adding the yeast—add it halfway through
the kneading process, rather than at the beginning, in
order to avoid overfermenting the dough. Bloom the
yeast in a few tablespoons of warm water, then add it to
the dough as you knead.

For recipes that already have 20- to 30-minute rest
periods between kneading sessions, you can add one
single rest period. For recipes without rest periods, the
dough can handle two 15- to 20-minute rest periods
spaced out over three kneading sessions.

IMPASTO
PER LA PIZZA
NAPOLETANA

Neapolitan-Style
Pizza Dough

*Makes enough dough for
four 12-inch pizzas*

---

590 grams (5 scant cups) bread flour,
plus more for dusting

1¾ grams (½ rounded teaspoon) active
dry yeast

380 grams (about 1½ cups) cold
filtered water

12 grams (2 teaspoons) sea salt

Thick-rimmed Neapolitan-style pizza has become synonymous with Italy, and it is arguably the country's most famous export. In Naples, as elsewhere, this popular food is baked in a domed wood-burning oven, but this recipe has been adapted for your home oven so you can enjoy the chewy crust and elastic dough of *pizza napoletana* in your own home—though if you can, take a trip to Naples, specifically Pizzeria da Attilio, 50 Kalò, and La Notizia, for the real deal. Plan ahead to make this pizza, as the cold, slow rise in the refrigerator takes at least 20 hours. Recipes for a classic Margherita pizza and three pizzas inspired by the south and its famed pizza makers follow.

In the bowl of a stand mixer fitted with the dough hook, combine the flour, yeast, and cold water. Mix on the lowest speed until the dough just comes together and there is no more dry flour in the bowl. Cover with plastic wrap and set aside to hydrate at room temperature for 30 minutes.

Return the bowl to the stand mixer and mix on medium-low speed. Add the salt and mix for 20 minutes more to build strength and until the dough is very smooth and elastic.

Turn the dough out onto a lightly floured work surface, shape it into a tight ball, and transfer to a lightly oiled bowl. Cover with plastic wrap and refrigerate at 39°F to 41°F for at least 20 hours and up to 30 hours.

Turn the dough out onto a lightly floured surface, allowing it to gently release from the bowl, and cut it into 4 equal pieces, weighing about 250 grams (9 ounces) each, with a dough scraper or knife.

Working with one piece of dough at a time, take the four corners and pull and fold them into the center to attach. Do not flatten. The dough will tighten up and take on a round shape. Flip the dough seam-side down. Place the palm of your hand on top of the ball, resting your thumb and pinkie against the sides and your other fingertips on the counter. Gently move the ball in circles, taking care to prevent any tears to create a tight, even ball. Repeat this process with the remaining dough pieces. Place the shaped dough balls on a greased baking sheet. Brush lightly with oil and cover the whole baking sheet with plastic wrap. Set aside at room temperature until the dough has nearly doubled in size, about 2 hours.

(recipe continues)

Forty-five minutes prior to baking, preheat the oven and broiler to high and set an inverted baking sheet or a baking stone on the second to highest rack to preheat as well.

Place one dough ball on a well-floured surface, then sprinkle more flour on top. Starting in the center, work the dough into a small disc by pushing your fingers flat into the dough, leaving the edge untouched. Flip over the disc and continue until you have a round disc about 8 inches in diameter.

To stretch the dough to the desired size, drape it over the back of your hands and knuckles, fingers bent inward. Gently rotate the dough, stretching it little by little until it is around 12 inches in diameter.

Transfer the shaped dough to a pizza peel or a parchment paper–lined inverted baking sheet. Top as directed in the recipe that follows, and transfer the pizza to the preheated baking sheet or baking stone (see Note). Bake until the crust is lightly charred around the edges and the toppings are cooked, 4 to 6 minutes. Repeat with the remaining dough balls, allowing the oven and the pizza stone or baking sheet to reheat for 10 to 15 minutes before baking the next pizza.

Serve immediately.

NOTE A baking stone will give your pizza a better crust, better volume, and incomparable lightness. If you do not have one, an inverted baking sheet or unglazed quarry tiles will work as substitutes. For the best results, preheat the stone or inverted baking sheet on the second rack from the top for at least 45 minutes before baking your pizza. Recipe cooking times depend upon your baking surface and will be shorter if you use a stone.

PIZZA MARGHERITA
Margherita Pizza
Makes one 12-inch pizza

The south's most iconic pizza features cow's-milk mozzarella, tomato sauce, and basil.

Dough for 1 pizza crust (page 189)

3½ ounces canned whole tomatoes

Sea salt

Pinch of dried oregano

2 tablespoons extra-virgin olive oil

4½ ounces mozzarella, cut into ½-inch cubes, excess water squeezed out

5 fresh basil leaves

Shape the dough as directed above.

Place the tomatoes in a medium bowl and blend with an immersion blender, or crush by hand, until they are broken down to a chunky puree. Season with salt, oregano, and 1 tablespoon of the olive oil.

Spoon the tomato sauce over the pizza dough to the edge of the raised border, then distribute the mozzarella evenly. Bake as directed above.

Garnish with the basil leaves and drizzle with the remaining 1 tablespoon olive oil.

PIZZA ALL'ALTO CASERTANO
Alto Casertano Pizza
Makes one 12-inch pizza

Inspired by Franco Pepe's dessert pizza at Pepe in Grani (see page 194), the toppings evoke the flavor of Franco's native subregion of Campania. Use the highest quality lard you can find.

Dough for 1 pizza crust (page 189)

1½ tablespoons lard

¼ cup fig jam

½ cup shaved Conciato Romano or Pecorino Romano

Freshly ground black pepper

Shape the dough as directed on page 192.

Spread the lard over the pizza dough to the edge of the raised border. Bake as directed on page 192.

Drizzle the fig jam over the melted lard, distribute the Conciato Romano shavings evenly, and season with pepper.

LA *MARINARA RIVISITATA DI ATTILIO BACHETTI*

Attilio's Marinara Pizza
Makes one 12-inch pizza

At Pizzeria da Attilio, a pizzeria in Naples that opened in 1938, *pizzaiolo* Attilio Bachetti customizes the traditional marinara pie, adding Pecorino Romano, Parmigiano-Reggiano, and basil leaves to the classic tomato and garlic toppings.

Dough for 1 pizza crust (page 189)

3½ ounces canned whole tomatoes

Sea salt

2 tablespoons extra-virgin olive oil

½ garlic clove, sliced paper thin

2 teaspoons finely grated Pecorino Romano

2 teaspoons finely grated Parmigiano-Reggiano

5 fresh basil leaves

Shape the dough as directed on page 192.

Place the tomatoes in a medium bowl and blend with an immersion blender, or crush by hand, until they are broken down to a chunky puree. Season with salt and 1 tablespoon of the olive oil. Spoon the tomato sauce over the pizza dough to the edge of the raised border, then distribute the garlic evenly. Bake as directed on page 192.

Sprinkle the pizza with the Pecorino Romano and Parmigiano-Reggiano, garnish with the basil leaves, and drizzle with the remaining 1 tablespoon olive oil.

PIZZA CON *'NDUJA E FIOR DI LATTE*

'Nduja and Mozzarella Pizza
Makes one 12-inch pizza

Calabrian ingredients meet Campanian ones on this pie topped with a spicy spreadable salami and mozzarella made from cow's milk.

Dough for 1 pizza crust (page 189)

2 ounces canned whole tomatoes

Sea salt

1 tablespoon extra-virgin olive oil

4½ ounces mozzarella, cut into ½-inch cubes, excess water squeezed out

3 ounces *'nduja*

5 fresh basil leaves

Shape the dough as directed on page 192.

Place the tomatoes in a medium bowl and blend with an immersion blender, or crush by hand, until they are broken down into a chunky puree. Season with salt and the olive oil. Spoon the tomato sauce over the pizza dough to the edge of the raised border, then distribute the mozzarella and *'nduja* evenly over the sauce. Bake as directed on page 192.

Garnish with the basil leaves.

La Pizza di Franco Pepe
Franco Pepe's Pizza

Pizza is never *just* pizza. Bits of history, culture, and politics are always woven into its glutinous strands. And in Caiazzo, a once declining village 30 miles from Naples in Campania's Alto Casertano subregion, pizza is life. The deity is Franco Pepe, a tall, lean vision in white, widely recognized as Italy's (and hence, the world's) greatest *pizzaiolo*. His pizzeria, Pepe in Grani, serves masterfully crafted, supremely delectable, highly digestible, thick-rimmed pizzas made from the best ingredients available. But its importance isn't limited to craft or flavor.

The pizzeria occupies a three-story stone building situated in a steep alley in Caiazzo's historical center. More than a few locals questioned Franco's sanity when he decided to open in what was then a desolate place. But the six hundred pizzas he serves on busy nights, coupled with the narrow alley packed daily with people waiting for tables, would seem to prove otherwise. Pepe in Grani has become a veritable pizza pilgrimage destination since it opened in 2012. Diners come from Naples, Rome, Milan, and beyond to eat Franco's pizzas. Their visits bring revenue to the town's shops, bars, and parking meters.

Pepe in Grani has also stimulated Alto Casertano's agricultural life. Franco works closely with small producers and local farms to obtain the ingredients for his pizzas and calzones. One of his greatest assets is Vincenzo Coppola, a young agronomist dedicated to discovering and preserving the biodiversity of the area. Together they are seeking to revive an indigenous grain dubbed *autonomia* that was abandoned in the 1950s. They recovered seeds from a ninety-year-old farmer, and now the grain is once again harvested and milled locally.

They also work with La Sbecciatrice farm to grow heirloom tomatoes like the *pomodoro riccio* and *vernino genuino,* as well as chickpeas and beans. Pepe tops his pizzas with these and other local products, like Letino potatoes, onions from Alife, and mozzarella from Il Casolare in Alvignano.

Each pizza Franco produces is the result of a set of choices: He and his team have chosen to highlight the natural bounty of their region. They have chosen to stay in Caiazzo in spite of the obstacles it presented initially and continues to present. They have chosen to forge responsible relationships with the land, their producers, and their clientele. Every pizza is the fruit of thoughtful planning, planting, producing, and harvesting, which respects the rhythms of nature and transmits flavor. It will simply change the way you think about food.

Go taste for yourself, and you'll see this is not hyperbole. Like I said, it's not just pizza.

FRISELLE

Italian Rusk

Makes 12 friselle

---

750 grams (6½ cups) type "2" flour, plus more for dusting

1 recipe *Friselle Biga* (recipe follows)

15 grams (2½ tablespoons) sea salt

3 grams (1 teaspoon) active dry yeast

575 grams (2½ cups) cold filtered water

Summers in the south are hot—and they're getting hotter. Home cooks there have to find a delicate balance between cooking from scratch and not fainting from heatstroke. In that spirit, they have devised recipes that minimize the amount of heat needed to prepare meals. *Friselle*, baked dough rings known for their long shelf life, are one such hack. They used to be eaten by sailors and fishermen who needed nonperishable foods for their long voyages. *Friselle* are twice-baked and designed to be too hard to eat on their own, so to make them palatable, they must be broken up, drizzled with water, and served with a flavorful seasonal topping. I love them with *capunata* (page 59) or with simple tomato and basil, but you can build your own.

To start, you'll need to prepare the *biga,* a type of pre-ferment, which gives a more complex flavor and a more desirable dough than would be achieved with active dry yeast alone. The *biga* must be made the day before you plan to bake the *friselle.*

In the bowl of a stand mixer fitted with the dough hook, combine the flour, *biga*, salt, yeast, and 400 grams (1¾ cups) of the cold water and mix on low until the water has been absorbed, about 5 minutes. With the mixer running, add the remaining water about 50 grams (¼ cup) at a time until it all has been incorporated, then mix for 3 minutes more to strengthen the dough.

Transfer the dough to a large, lightly oiled bowl. Brush with oil and cover with plastic wrap. Set aside to rise in the warmest part of your kitchen until it has almost doubled in size, about 2 hours.

Preheat the oven to 475°F.

Transfer the dough to a lightly floured work surface. Divide the dough into 6 equal pieces using a dough scraper or a knife. Gently roll each piece into a ball. Dust with flour, cover with a clean kitchen towel, and allow to rest for 20 to 30 minutes.

Using your thumb and index finger, gently poke a hole in the center of each dough ball and gently stretch the dough to resemble the size and shape of a large bagel. Set on a lightly floured baking sheet and allow to rest for 20 minutes.

Bake the *friselle* until hard and lightly golden, 15 to 18 minutes. Remove the *friselle* from the oven and set aside to cool. Reduce the oven temperature to 400°F. When the *friselle* are cool, slice them in half as though you are halving a bagel. Return to the oven and bake, halves separated, working in batches as needed, until they are crispy and fully dried, 10 to 15 minutes. Set aside to cool. To serve, break into pieces, soften with a few tablespoons of water, and serve with the toppings of your choice.

Friselle Biga
Makes enough for 12 *friselle*

60 grams (2 ounces) filtered water

90 grams (¾ cup) bread flour

⅛ gram (pinch) active dry yeast

Neutral oil (see page 37), for greasing

In the bowl of a stand mixer fitted with the dough hook, add the water, then the flour, then the yeast. Mix for 5 minutes on medium speed. The dough should be fairly dry. Transfer the *biga* to a lightly oiled bowl, cover with plastic wrap, and refrigerate for 2 hours.

Remove the *biga* from the refrigerator and allow it to ferment at room temperature for 10 to 12 hours, until it doubles in size. Use as directed in the recipe.

PANE DI MATERA

Matera-Style Durum
Wheat Bread

Makes two 10-inch loaves

---

150 grams (5.3 ounces) 50% hydration
Lievito Madre (page 205)

430 grams (1¾ cups plus 1 tablespoon)
filtered water

600 grams (3½ cups) *farina di semola
rimacinata* (fancy durum flour; see
page 203), plus more for dusting

1¾ grams (½ rounded teaspoon) active
dry yeast

13 grams (2 rounded teaspoons)
sea salt

Neutral oil (see page 37), for greasing

This bread made from *farina di semola rimacinata* (see page 203) is named for Matera, an ancient city in eastern Basilicata close to vast grain fields. For centuries, bakers have milled durum wheat and fermented it using sourdough starter. The shape of the loaf is unique to each bakery, but all make three incisions in the surface of the dough before baking to represent the Holy Trinity. You will need to prepare a sourdough starter hydrated to 50 percent at least a week ahead of baking the bread. One hundred percent semolina loaves can be challenging for beginners, but practice makes perfect!

In the bowl of a stand mixer, combine the starter with 360 grams (1½ cups) of the filtered water and set aside for 5 minutes to hydrate, then break up, partly dissolve, and mix using your hands or a wooden spoon. Fit the mixer with the dough hook and add the *farina di semola rimacinata* to the bowl. Mix on low speed until there is no more dry *farina di semola rimacinata* in the bowl, about 2 minutes. Cover the bowl with plastic wrap and allow the dough to rest for 30 minutes. This helps with the hydration of the very hard *farina di semola rimacinata* granules and will help them attain elasticity.

Add the yeast to the bowl and mix on low speed for 25 minutes, slowly adding the salt and remaining water, alternating the two, over the course of 5 minutes. Increase the speed to medium and mix for 5 minutes more. The dough should be smooth, elastic, and somewhat shiny.

Turn the dough out onto a lightly floured work surface, shape into a ball, and place in a lightly oiled bowl. Cover with plastic wrap. Set aside to rise at room temperature until the dough doubles in size, about 1¾ hours.

Turn the dough out onto a floured work surface, allowing it to gently release from the bowl. Using your fingertips, press down gently to deflate. Divide the dough into two equal pieces using a dough scraper or a knife. Working with one piece of dough, grasp one side and fold it two thirds of the way across the dough, then fold the opposing side over the first flap like a letter. Starting at the short end facing you, roll the dough away from you into a loose roll.

Position the dough so the seam is facing downward. Press down gently so the seam closes. Repeat with the second piece of dough.

(recipe continues)

Transfer both pieces of dough to a floured baking sheet. Lightly dust the surface of the dough with flour and cover the baking sheet tightly with plastic wrap. Set the dough aside to rise at room temperature until it has doubled in size, about 1 hour.

Preheat the oven to 480°F. Set a baking stone or an inverted baking sheet on the center rack to preheat as well.

When the dough has risen, transfer it to a lightly floured work surface, seam-side up. Sprinkle a little bit of flour over the dough. Working with one piece of dough at a time, press down gently on the dough to deflate it partially, working the dough into a rectangular shape measuring about 10 × 8 inches and 1 inch thick. Starting with one of the shorter sides, fold in the four corners until they meet in the middle. Roll one corner of the folded rectangle toward the center of the dough. Stop before reaching the center. Turn the dough 180 degrees and repeat with the opposing corner. You should now have two "rolls" connected by a thinner piece of dough in the middle. With the side of your hand, press down on the center piece to compact it. Fold one of the "rolls" over the center piece and press it against the other "roll." You should now have two stacked rolls. Press down slightly on the rolls and press hard on the thinner piece connecting the rolls.

Dust the loaves with a little bit of flour and cover with plastic wrap on the work surface. Allow to rest for 15 minutes.

When the loaves have rested, uncover them and, using a sharp knife, make three vertical cuts at equal distance in the side where the "rolls" are joined together. Transfer the loaves to a pizza peel or a parchment paper–lined inverted baking sheet (see page 192). Reshape them slightly by curving the ends to form a crescent shape, opening the cuts somewhat.

Transfer the loaves (including the parchment paper, if using an inverted baking sheet) onto the preheated baking sheet or baking stone in the oven. Spray with a bit of water to create some steam and immediately close the oven door.

Bake for 5 minutes, then reduce the oven temperature to 420°F. Bake until the loaves are very dark brown, feel light, and sound hollow when tapped on the underside, about 1 hour.

There are thousands of grain varieties in the world and many of them arrived in Italy from the east in the Iron Age. Grains were grown for feeding animals and milling to make flour for bread baking—and even a little pasta making. Today, grain is milled into flour throughout Italy in a range of settings, from large industrial complexes to small, artisanal operations, and even in homes. While the types of grains—and therefore flours—may not be identical to those outside Italy, as long as you know how flour works, you can execute authentic South Italian doughs wherever you are.

All-Purpose Flour

As the name implies, all-purpose flour is a versatile product that can be used in a range of recipes. That's not to say it's the best flour for all recipes, though. It's milled to be white and tasteless, so it's not ideal for bread baking, for which you want the raw ingredients to impart flavor and character, but it's just fine for making piecrusts and simple doughs that will be filled or paired with something with a lot of its own flavor.

Bread Flour

Bread flour's name is also descriptive. It is relatively high in protein—it averages between 11 percent and 14 percent—making it suitable for bread-baking because the protein imparts strength and facilitates rising, enabling the dough to stretch as it traps air in its gluten network during fermentation. It is often made from a blend of different grains that are milled separately, then mixed together to create a flour with the necessary characteristics for achieving a reliable bread dough. Using bread flour in the pizza dough recipe on page 189 results in a chewier-than-normal crust, which is critical for replicating the signature texture of *pizza napoletana* (page 189).

Durum Wheat Flour

Durum wheat, referred to as semolina or *semola di grano duro*, is used in bread baking and pasta making and tends to be high in protein, often coming in at around 14 percent. *Durum* means "hard" in Latin, and durum's hardness makes it great for achieving an al dente "bite" in cooked pasta doughs. Its gluten network, created when flour is hydrated, lacks elasticity, however, so it can make strong, short, thick pasta shapes like orecchiette (see page 90) and *carrati* (see page 92) but isn't great for long, thin pasta strands that need to "stretch."

In Italy, durum wheat flour takes on a number of forms. *Semolino* is a really coarse grind and is used for porridges, desserts, and couscous-like pastas. *Farina di semola* is ground to medium fineness, has a deep yellow color, a lot of flavor, and is used for making pasta. *Farina di semola rimacinata*, on the other hand, is fine, whiter than *farina di semola*, and is ideal for baking. In the US, *farina di semola* is called semolina flour or pasta flour. Meanwhile, durum flour may be coarse like *farina di semola* or fine like *farina di semola rimacinata*. To be sure you are chosing the correct flour for baking, look for so-called fancy durum flour, which is *farina di semola rimacinata*.

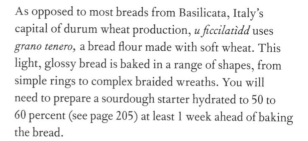

U FICCILATÌDD

Fennel Seed Bread

Makes one 10-inch bread ring

100 grams (3½ ounces) 50 to
60% hydration firm mature *Lievito Madre* (page 205)

125 grams (½ cup) filtered water

290 grams (1¾ cups plus
2 tablespoons) bread flour

15 grams (1 tablespoon) extra-virgin
olive oil

8 grams (1½ tablespoons) sea salt

2 grams (1 teaspoon) fennel seeds

As opposed to most breads from Basilicata, Italy's capital of durum wheat production, *u ficcilatìdd* uses *grano tenero*, a bread flour made with soft wheat. This light, glossy bread is baked in a range of shapes, from simple rings to complex braided wreaths. You will need to prepare a sourdough starter hydrated to 50 to 60 percent (see page 205) at least 1 week ahead of baking the bread.

In the bowl of a stand mixer fitted with the paddle attachment, combine the starter, filtered water, and 80 grams (½ cup) of the flour. Mix on low speed until the mixture is smooth and creamy, about 2 minutes. Cover the bowl and set aside for 20 minutes.

Fit the mixer with the dough hook. Add the olive oil, salt, fennel seeds, and the remaining flour to the sourdough mixture. Mix on medium speed for 12 minutes. The dough will become smooth, firm, and silky.

Turn the dough onto an unfloured work surface. Roll into a 6 × 16-inch rectangle. Brush the surface with a bit of water.

Starting from the long end closest to you, roll the dough away from you as tightly as possible, forming a tight 16-inch-long roll. Seal the seam by pinching the dough. Join the ends of the roll and pinch together to form a ring.

Place the dough ring on a baking sheet lined with parchment and cover tightly with plastic wrap. Place in the refrigerator at 39°F to 41°F to cold-rise for at least 12 hours and up to 16 hours.

Remove from the refrigerator and place the baking sheet in a fairly warm place (77°F to 86°F) to rise until it has doubled in size, 4 to 6 hours.

Preheat the oven to 425°F with a rack in the center position.

Using a sharp knife, make four cuts about ½ inch deep into the surface of the dough. The ends of the incisions should touch, forming a rectangle in the ring. Spray the dough with water and transfer to the oven. Bake for 10 minutes, then reduce the oven temperature to 390°F and bake for 20 minutes more or until the bread sounds hollow when tapped on the bottom.

Transfer to a wire rack and let cool to room temperature before serving. Slice and serve with *U Morzeddhu e Baccalà* (page 129).

Lievito Madre

Sourdough Starter

500 grams (17.6 ounces) bread flour

500 grams (17.6 ounces) whole rye flour

Filtered water, at room temperature

In a large resealable container, combine the flours.

In a small glass bowl, combine 100 grams (3½ ounces) filtered water and 100 grams (3½ ounces) of the flour mixture and mix until smooth. Cover with a clean kitchen towel and allow the mixture to sit at room temperature for 48 hours.

Begin to check for signs of fermentation, such as bubbles on the surface and around the edges of the mixture. Cover and allow to sit for another 24 hours. Check again to confirm that the bubbling has intensified. You should be able to smell the wonderfully musty and acidic aromas of fermentation.

Place 25 grams (.88 ounce) of the fermented starter in a small bowl, discarding the remainder. Add 1.76 ounces (50 grams) of filtered water and 1.76 ounces (50 grams) of the reserved flour mixture and mix well. Cover and allow to sit at warm room temperature for 24 hours. Repeat the feeding and discarding process once more.

To hydrate to 50 to 60 percent, place 50 grams (1.76 ounces) of the starter in a small bowl and add 50 grams (1.76 ounces) of room-temperature filtered water and 110 grams (3.88 ounces) of the flour mixture. Knead it together into a smooth dough. Cover and allow to sit at room temperature for 12 hours.

Place 50 grams (1.76 ounces) of the fermented starter in a small bowl, discarding the remainder. Add 50 grams (1.76 ounces) of room-temperature filtered water and 100 grams (3.5 ounces) of the flour mixture. Repeat the discarding and feeding process every 12 hours for about 1 week. You will observe the rise and fall cycle: volume will increase after feeding, then decrease. The aromas will change as well: at first funky and acidic, followed by pleasantly sour aromas reminiscent of yogurt. On the day prior to using, feed the starter twice, 12 hours apart.

To make bread with another kind of flour (semolina, for example), make the two last feedings before baking with that particular flour instead of the flour mix.

Continue to perpetuate the remaining sourdough following the same base recipe of 50 grams (1.76 ounces) mature sourdough starter blended with 50 grams (1.76 ounces) of filtered water and 100 grams (3.5 ounces) of the flour blend every 12 hours. If you're not baking for a few days or can't maintain your sourdough starter, you can slow down the fermentation process through refrigeration. First, feed the starter normally, leave it for 2 hours at room temperature, then transfer to the refrigerator. You can feed the starter this way every 48 hours. Just be sure to do at least two 12-hour room-temperature feeding cycles prior to using.

To scale up the recipe, adjust the discarding and feeding amounts. For example, to make 400 grams (14.1 ounces) of starter, combine 100 grams (3.5 ounces) of the starter with 100 grams (3.5 ounces) of water and 200 grams (7 ounces) of flour blend. Allow the starter to mature for 4 to 8 hours, until doubled in size following a feeding, before using.

NOTE To make a successful sourdough starter, forget about cup measurements and weigh everything on a kitchen scale.

'A PIZZA CO'
L'ERVA

Vegetable Calzone

Serves 8

FOR THE DOUGH

500 grams (4 cups) all-purpose flour, plus more for dusting

2½ grams (1 rounded teaspoon) active dry yeast

11 grams (2 rounded teaspoons) sea salt

70 grams (¼ cup plus 1 tablespoon) extra-virgin olive oil

200 grams (¾ cup plus 1 scant tablespoon) filtered water

FOR THE FILLING

Sea salt

1,000 grams (2 pounds) mixed greens (Swiss chard, collard greens, kale, spinach)

60 grams (¼ cup) extra-virgin olive oil, plus more as needed

1 garlic clove, smashed

5 small anchovy fillets, cleaned (see page 134)

25 grams (3 tablespoons) pine nuts

25 grams (3 tablespoons) raisins

75 grams (¼ cup) Gaeta olives, pitted and roughly chopped

Freshly ground black pepper

Deep in the heart of Irpinia, a rural region in the southeastern part of Campania, Good Friday is commemorated with solemn processions and lean meals. Because Christ was crucified on a Friday, the Catholic Church implemented a meatless diet on all Fridays out of respect, which meant fish and vegetable dishes were the only permissible ones. The rule was loosened in the 1960s, but meatless vegetable pies are still a staple in the region, and while the wild greens mix changes from house to house, you're likely to find the last winter escarole and the first spring greens, like Swiss chard and spinach, baked with a sweet-and-savory mix of pine nuts, raisins, and anchovies.

Make the dough: In the bowl of a stand mixer fitted with the dough hook, combine the flour, yeast, salt, olive oil, and water. Mix on low speed until there is no more dry flour in the bowl, about 3 minutes. Increase the speed to medium-low and mix for 12 minutes. If mixing by hand (see page 187), knead for at least 15 minutes.

Turn the dough out onto a lightly floured work surface and form into a tight ball. Return the dough to the bowl, cover with plastic wrap, and allow it to sit at room temperature until it has at least doubled in size, about 2½ hours.

Make the filling: Bring a large pot of water to a boil over high heat. Salt the water (see page 31). When the salt has dissolved, blanch the greens until soft, 2 to 5 minutes, depending on the type. Work in batches as needed, allowing the water to return to a boil before adding the next batch. Drain and spread the greens out on a baking sheet to cool for 20 minutes. When cool enough to handle, gently squeeze out any excess water and chop the greens into 1-inch pieces.

Heat the olive oil in a large skillet over medium heat. When the oil begins the shimmer, add the garlic and anchovies and cook until the garlic just turns golden and the anchovies melt into the oil, about 3 minutes. Add the pine nuts and cook for about 1 minute. Add the greens, raisins, and olives. Season with salt and pepper. Cook for 5 to 10 minutes, until the greens are cooked through. Remove the skillet from the heat and spread out the mixture to cool to room temperature.

Assemble the pizza: Preheat the oven to 410°F with racks in the center and lowest positions. Lightly grease a 9-inch springform pan with olive oil.

Divide the dough into two unequal pieces, about two thirds and one third. Roll out the larger piece of dough on a well-floured surface to a thickness of about 3 millimeters (⅛ inch) and a diameter of at least 16 inches. Transfer it to the prepared pan, gently pressing it into the corners and up the sides, repairing any holes. The dough should overhang the sides of the pan. Meanwhile, roll out the smaller piece of the dough to the same thickness, then use a knife or pastry wheel to cut it to the dimensions of the pan.

Transfer the vegetable mixture into the dough-lined pan, spreading it into an even, compact layer. Fit the second piece of the dough over the vegetables. Brush the edge of the top piece of dough with water and fold the overhanging dough over it, pressing gently to seal. Cover and allow to rise at room temperature for 20 minutes.

Brush the dough all over with olive oil. Make a small hole in the center of the dough and prick with a fork all over.

Bake the pizza for 10 minutes on the lowest rack, then brush a second time with olive oil. This will give the crust a little extra shine when baked, but there won't yet be any visual difference in the dough. Drizzle more oil around the pizza between the dough and the pan. Transfer the pizza to the center rack, reduce the oven temperature to 350°F, and bake for 25 minutes more, until the crust is lightly browned. Remove from the oven and allow to rest for at least 30 minutes before removing from the pan, then let cool to room temperature on a wire rack before slicing.

DOLCI

—

DESSERTS

U' PISCQUETT'L

Lemon Zest and
Cherry Jam Cookies

Makes 30 cookies

---

1 pound almond flour

⅓ cup sugar

⅓ cup honey

Zest of 1 lemon

¼ cup *rosolio all'arancia* or *Limoncello*
(page 233)

2 eggs, beaten

1 cup cherry jam

Midway between Brindisi and Taranto, Ceglie Messapica is an ancient village rising on a plateau overlooking the olive groves and rolling hills of central Puglia. The town's signature cookie, called *u' piscquett'l* in the local dialect and *biscotti di Ceglie* in Italian, uses almond flour, a common ingredient in the south's sweets, as the base of its dough, which is flavored with lemon zest and an orange liqueur called *rosolio all'arancia*. Traditionally, the cookies are filled with cherry jam made from fruit harvested in the late spring, but you can use any fruit jam you wish.

Preheat the oven to 350°F. Line two baking sheets with parchment paper.

In a large bowl, stir together the almond flour, sugar, honey, and lemon zest until thoroughly combined. Add the *rosolio* and the eggs. Using your hands or a wooden spoon, mix the dough in the bowl until all the liquid is incorporated. The dough should be tacky but not wet.

Take a fistful of the dough in your hand and press it onto a parchment paper–covered surface until it is a ½ inch thick and 2 × 4 inches wide. Spoon the cherry jam onto the center of the dough lengthwise, then, using the parchment paper to assist you, "wrap" the dough around the jam, rolling it into a log like sushi. Unwrap and slice crosswise into 1-inch-thick rounds. Repeat the parchment rolling and slicing with the remaining dough and jam.

Place the slices on the prepared baking sheets, spaced at least ½ inch apart, and bake until the cookies begin to turn golden, 15 minutes. The cookies will keep in a sealed container at room temperature for up to 1 week.

CROSTATA DI ROTONDA

Jam Tart with Lard Crust

Serves 8 to 10

7 ounces pork lard

¾ cup plus 2 tablespoons sugar

3 egg yolks

4 ounces sweet vermouth

4 cups all-purpose flour, plus more for dusting

1 teaspoon baking soda

Unsalted butter, for greasing

1¼ cups sour cherry jam

½ cup roughly chopped walnuts

Nicola Romano's black pigs forage for food on his dozens of acres of land deep in northern Calabria's Parco Nazionale della Sila. Trained as an accountant, Nicola found his passion for nature steering him away from his desk; today he raises Nero Calabrese pigs, a nearly extinct indigenous species. He works his animals into *'nduja*, *soppressata*, and other chile-laced *salumi* under his family home in Acri. His friend Franca Cozzolino oversees the operation, and though she has a flair for grinding and seasoning meat, she's also a talented baker. This is her famous crostata recipe, made with the rich rendered fat of Nicola's Calabrese pigs, but you can use any high-quality lard, ideally from sustainably raised heritage pigs.

In the bowl of a stand mixer fitted with the paddle attachment, beat the lard and sugar on medium speed until light and creamy, about 3 minutes. Scrape down the sides of the bowl with a rubber spatula, then add the egg yolks and vermouth and beat on medium speed until incorporated. Add the flour and baking soda and mix on low speed until the dough just begins to come together, about 1 minute. Scrape down the sides of the bowl and the paddle attachment and mix until the dough comes together and all the ingredients are incorporated, about 30 seconds more.

Turn the dough out onto a lightly floured surface. Using your hands, gather the dough into a mass and, using a sharp knife or pastry cutter, divide it into two unequal pieces, about two thirds and one third. Wrap each piece in plastic wrap and chill in the refrigerator for 1 hour or up to 3 or 4 days. (If you chill the dough for longer than 1 hour, allow it to sit at room temperature for 30 minutes before using.)

Preheat the oven to 350°F. Lightly grease a 10-inch springform pan or fluted tart pan with butter.

Roll out the larger piece of dough between two lightly floured sheets of parchment paper to a diameter of 15 inches and a thickness of ¼ to ⅛ inch. Transfer it to the prepared pan, gently pressing it into the corners and up the sides; if you're using a springform pan, the dough should come about ¾ inch up the sides. Repair any tears. Refrigerate until firm, about 30 minutes.

(recipe continues)

La Cultura del Caffè
Coffee Culture

Coffee only landed in Italy about three and a half centuries ago, but that's plenty of time for the caffeinated drink to have become the south's most iconic nonalcoholic beverage. Although coffee beans are indigenous to Ethiopia, they moved into Eastern Europe, then Central Europe, via the Ottoman Empire. Ethiopia remains a major producer of coffee, but production has also expanded to South and Central America, and today, most of Italy's beans come from South America rather than East Africa. Regardless of provenance, to produce Italian-style coffee, the beans are harvested, dried, roasted, and finally ground before being forced through a machine with water.

Coffee is particularly synonymous with Naples, where Gran Caffè La Caffettiera in Piazza dei Martiri and Caffè Gambrinus overlooking the Royal Palace and Piazza del Plebiscito still retain their gilded unification era interiors. Meanwhile, Mexico, the coffee shop owned by the Passalacqua roasting company, has locations all over town dripping in coffee kitsch dating to the 1950s.

Regardless of setting, whether it's a formal coffee house or a casual café, the price of an espresso hovers around 1 euro, making it an affordable necessity for most. At every time of day, patrons crowd around busy counters awaiting their orders, which drip into preheated cups—locals claim it's more gentle on the hot coffee than a room temperature cup would be.

The most common coffee in the south is espresso and its name says it all: water is *expressed* through a machine, and it's meant to be made and consumed quickly. It is served *amaro* (without sugar) or *zuccherato* (with sugar), and can be made *macchiato* (spiked with a bit of steamed milk). Milk-based coffees also include cappuccino (espresso accompanied by a generous amount of frothed milk) and *caffè latte* (warmed milk with a shot of espresso added). The large-format, syrup-laced, Starbucks-style coffees haven't reached the south yet, so the most elaborate caffeinated drink you'll encounter will be a *caffè marocchino* (espresso layered with cocoa powder and steamed milk).

While none of these coffees is unique to the south, one coffee-related custom is *caffè sospeso,* a Neapolitan tradition of covering the cost of a coffee for a future client who can't afford it, a tacit acknowledgment that in Naples, coffee is a right and not a privilege.

MAKING THE LATTICE

In South Italy, pastry shops don't make lattices the way they do in the United States. They simply lay down the strips in one direction, then place a perpendicular layer on top. This method is perfectly acceptable and authentic, plus lard-based dough is sometimes difficult to weave.

Meanwhile, roll out the smaller piece of the dough to the same thickness, then use a pastry wheel or sharp knife to cut it into 1-inch-wide strips. Freeze the strips until firm, about 5 minutes.

Remove the pan from the refrigerator, then spread the cherry jam over the chilled dough. Use the dough strips to create a simple lattice (see left) on top. Trim any loose ends of the strips to fit the pan and pinch them to adhere to the edges of the bottom crust. Sprinkle over the walnuts.

Bake until golden brown all over, about 40 minutes. Transfer to a wire rack to cool before unmolding, about 30 minutes. Serve immediately or wrap in aluminum foil and store at room temperature for up to 1 week.

PIGNA DI PASQUA

Easter Pound Cake

Makes one 15-inch cake,
to serve 8 to 10

Until the 1960s in Cerreto Sannita in the interior of Campania, *la pigna* was prepared by women for their fiancés before Easter Sunday and presented on the morning of the holiday in order to demonstrate the women's talents and value. Decoration became a way for women to express themselves and compete against one another, and accordingly, it was quite elaborate. These days, the tradition of gifting the cake to one's future husband is long gone, but the *pigna* lives on in Cerreto's bakeries, where it is sold brushed with a simple glaze.

FOR THE PIGNA BIGA

3½ ounces (100 grams) lukewarm
   water

1½ teaspoons active dry yeast

1 cup all-purpose flour

FOR THE PIGNA

5 eggs

1¼ cup granulated sugar

5 cups all-purpose flour

6 ounces extra-virgin olive oil

3 ounces dry white wine

3 ounces Liquore Strega

Zest and juice of 1 lemon

Zest of 1 orange

1 teaspoon aniseeds

Unsalted butter, for greasing

Make the *Pigna Biga*: Pour the warm water into a small bowl and sprinkle the yeast over top. Set aside for a few minutes, until the yeast has dissolved. Stir in the flour until it forms a soft dough. Cover with plastic wrap and allow the mixture to ferment at room temperature overnight, or 10 to 12 hours.

Make the *Pigna*: In the bowl of a stand mixer fitted with the paddle attachment, beat the eggs and sugar on medium speed until light and creamy, about 3 minutes. Scrape down the sides of the bowl with a rubber spatula, then add the flour, olive oil, white wine, Strega, lemon zest, lemon juice, orange zest, and aniseeds. Beat on medium speed until incorporated, about 2 minutes. Add the *Pigna Biga* and beat on medium speed for 5 minutes more.

Grease a 15-inch Bundt pan or high-sided 10-inch springform pan.

Scrape the mixture into the Bundt pan. Cover with plastic wrap and set aside to rise in a warm place until doubled in size, 4 to 6 hours.

Preheat the oven to 350°F.

Unwrap and bake until cooked through and browned, about 35 minutes. Let cool before unmolding, about 45 minutes. The *pigna* will keep in a sealed container at room temperature for about 1 week.

GIURGIULENA

Calabrian Sesame-Nut
Brittle

Makes about twenty 2-inch squares

Unsalted butter, for greasing

5 tablespoons sugar

1½ cups (about 16 ounces) honey
(I like orange blossom honey)

1 pound sesame seeds

4½ ounces almonds, raw and
unbleached

Zest of 1 orange

1 teaspoon ground cinnamon

2 tablespoons colored sprinkles

The eighth-century Arab conquest of the south brought new ingredients and sweets to the Italian peninsula (see page 159). One of these, called *cupetta* in the Benevento and Salentino dialects and *giurgiulena* in Castrovillari, Calabria, is made with sugar, honey, and sesame seeds. This long-lasting nut brittle was traditionally served around Christmastime, spooned onto washed orange leaves, but today it is sliced into bars. The sprinkles add color and a festive flair that is common in the sweets of the south. This recipe comes from La Locanda di Alia in Castrovillari, Calabria, where Daniela Alia makes them for the holiday season.

Grease parchment paper with butter and set aside on a large baking sheet.

In a large, deep pan, combine the sugar and honey over medium heat. When the sugar has dissolved into the honey, add the sesame seeds and cook, stirring frequently, until the seeds turn a shade darker, about 15 minutes. Add the almonds and continue to cook, stirring frequently, for 5 minutes more.

Remove the pan from the heat. Stir in the orange zest and cinnamon and set aside until the mixture is cool enough to handle.

Carefully pour the mixture onto the prepared parchment. While it's still warm, use a heatproof spatula to flatten the mixture to ½-inch thickness. Scatter the colored sprinkles over the mixture and lightly press them in with your fingertips. While still warm, cut into 2-inch diamonds on a diagonal using a sharp knife. Set aside to cool completely.

Giurgiulena will keep in a sealed container at room temperature for several months.

PASTORELLE

Chestnut-and-Chocolate-
Filled Christmas Cookies

Makes 20 pastorelle

FOR THE FILLING

½ cup heavy cream

4½ ounces dark chocolate, chopped

8 ounces chestnut puree, passed
    through a fine-mesh strainer

¼ cup granulated sugar

Zest of ½ lemon

FOR THE DOUGH

1 pound all-purpose flour

½ cup granulated sugar

1 tablespoon extra-virgin olive oil

1 cup water, plus more as needed

Neutral oil (see page 37), for frying

¼ cup confectioners' sugar

¼ cup unsweetened cocoa powder

Pastorelle are so-called because they would be made by daughters of *pastori* (shepherds) when they got engaged. The cookies were evidently so popular, they became a Christmas treat all over Cilento's Vallo di Diano, and especially in Cuccaro Vetere. They are shaped with four points to symbolize the star that attracted the Magi to Bethlehem.

Make the filling: In a medium saucepan, heat the cream over low heat, stirring to prevent scalding, until very hot and steaming but not boiling. Place the chocolate in a large bowl. Pour the cream over the chocolate and allow it to sit for about 2 minutes to melt the chocolate, then stir until smooth and well combined.

Add the chestnut puree, granulated sugar, and lemon zest to the chocolate and, using a handheld mixer, beat until creamy, about 2 minutes. Cover with plastic wrap and chill in the refrigerator for at least 2 hours before using.

Make the dough: Pour the flour and sugar onto a work surface and make a well in the middle. Add the olive oil and water to the well. Mix by hand, working from the edges into the center to gradually incorporate the ingredients. Add more water as needed to create a smooth, soft dough. Knead the dough until incorporated. Allow to rest at room temperature for about 30 minutes. Divide the dough into 4 equal pieces. Working with one piece at a time, roll the dough into a ⅛-inch-thick sheet. Using a circular cookie cutter or the rim of a juice glass, cut the dough into forty 3-inch rounds.

Spoon a tablespoon of the chestnut filling onto half the dough rounds. Cover each with one of the remaining dough rounds. Press the edges of the dough rounds together around the filling, taking care to fit the top layer tightly around the filling. Using your index finger and thumb, pinch the sides of the sealed dough into four points.

In a medium frying pan or cast-iron skillet, heat 2 inches of oil to 350°F. Line a baking sheet with paper towels.

Fry the cookies, working in batches as needed, until evenly golden brown, turning once, about 5 minutes total. Drain on the lined baking sheet. Serve dusted with confectioners' sugar and cocoa powder. The *pastorelle* will keep in a sealed container at room temperature for up to 3 days.

'MPIGNE

Potato Cookies

Makes 30 cookies

2 ounces warm water

3 teaspoons active dry yeast

4½ cups plus 2 tablespoons all-purpose
flour

3 eggs

1 cup granulated sugar

⅓ pound potatoes (I like russets),
boiled, peeled, and mashed

¼ cup whole milk

Zest of 1 lemon

1 vanilla bean, split lengthwise and
seeds scraped out

Pinch sea salt

½ cup (1 stick) unsalted butter,
at room temperature

Potatoes thrive in the sandy soil of Molise's mountainous land. The tuber is so abundant that it finds its way into every corner of the kitchen, including cookies. These ring-shaped, vanilla-scented potato cookies are a simple sweet for concluding a meal and pair well with an espresso or even a digestif.

Pour the warm water into a medium bowl and sprinkle the yeast over top. Set aside for a few minutes, until the yeast has dissolved. Add ½ cup plus 2 tablespoons of the flour and stir to incorporate. Cover with plastic wrap and set aside to rise in a warm place until doubled in size, about 1 hour.

Meanwhile, in the bowl of a stand mixer fitted with the paddle attachment, beat together the eggs and sugar on medium speed until smooth, about 2 minutes. Add the potatoes, milk, lemon zest, vanilla bean seeds, salt, and butter. Add the remaining 4 cups flour, 1 cup at a time, beating on medium speed to eliminate lumps after each addition. Add the yeast mixture and beat together on medium speed for 5 minutes. Cover the bowl with plastic wrap and set aside to rise until doubled in size.

Preheat the oven to 350°F. Line two baking sheets with parchment paper.

Working in batches using floured hands, roll the dough into ½-inch-thick ropes. Cut the ropes into 5-inch pieces, shape each piece into a ring by connecting the ends, and place the rings on the prepared baking sheets about 2 inches apart. Cover with a clean kitchen towel and set aside to rise for 30 minutes.

Beat the egg yolk and brush it over the rested 'mpigne. Bake until golden brown, about 15 minutes. Let cool completely in the pans or on a wire rack.

The cookies will keep in a sealed container at room temperature for up to 1 week.

La Frutta
Fruit as Dessert

I'll never forget my first visit to Puglia. I went home with a friend to visit his family. We nearly suffocated on the overnight train from Rome—even in the oppressive August heat, southbound travelers prefer stifling air to open windows, fearing a draft on their sweaty necks could cause a *colpo di vento* (literally "a strike from the wind," a widely feared affliction in the south).

My friend's father picked us up at the station; he was a psychologist by occupation, but I am certain he could have earned a living foraging for fruits and herbs. Over the course of our trip, he rarely drove a mile without pulling over and plucking a dozen warm figs from a strangers' field or grabbing prickly pears from a cluster of cacti with his bare, caloused hands. Each day at lunch and dinner, he would diligently peel the fruit, distributing plump figs or fluorescent pink prickly pears or whatever else to everyone at the table.

I learned some important things on that trip. One was that I could re-create many recipes of the south wherever I was—my *Cozze Ripiene* (page 119) tastes identical to the one my friend's mother makes. But another was that eating a single piece of fruit plucked fresh can be more satisfying than any cake, wedge of chocolate, or bowlful of gelato. And to experience that, you *must* visit the south.

MANDORLACCIO

Country-Style
Almond Cake

Serves 8 to 10

5 eggs, separated

½ cup sugar

Pinch of sea salt

2 cups almond flour

1 tablespoon honey

2 ounces almond praline, roughly
chopped

In Puglia, almond trees aren't quite as common as olive trees, but they are pretty close. The tree's fruit (the almond) emerges in a fuzzy green husk that dries out and turns brown as it matures. The almond within can be eaten raw, dried, or toasted and appears in both sweet and savory dishes across the region. Ground almonds can be used to make almond meal or almond flour (the distinction being that almond flour is generally ground from blanched almonds). *Mandorlaccio,* a flourless cake from Ruvo di Puglia, a village near Bari, uses almond flour instead of wheat flour and is one of many nut-based gluten-free cakes from the south.

Preheat the oven to 350°F. Line a 9-inch cake pan with parchment paper.

In a large bowl using a handheld mixer, beat the egg yolks, sugar, and salt until smooth. Add the almond flour and the honey and beat until combined.

In a medium bowl using clean beaters, beat the egg whites until stiff. Fold a third of the egg whites into the almond mixture with a spatula. Add the remaining egg whites, folding gently from the bottom until fully incorporated. Pour the batter into the prepared pan and sprinkle evenly with the almond praline.

Bake until cooked through and a toothpick inserted into the center comes out clean, about 30 minutes. Allow the cake to cool in the pan before unmolding, about 30 minutes.

The cake will keep in a sealed container at room temperature for up to a week.

LINGUE DI PROCIDA

Lemon Cream–Filled Puff Pastry

Makes 10 lingue

2 egg yolks

¼ cup granulated sugar, plus more
for dusting

2 tablespoons cornstarch

Pinch of sea salt

¾ cup whole milk

Zest of 1 lemon

1 pound Puff Pastry, homemade
(page 228) or store-bought

1 egg white, beaten

While many visitors to Naples hightail it to Capri or Ischia, my favorite island in the bay is Procida, a comparatively small volcanic crescent that's home to a few pretty pastel-hued fishing villages and a handful of volcanic sand beaches. I like to stay in the middle of the island, above the stunning Chiaiolella beach, and every morning I walk to the port 30 minutes away for a *lingua*, the island's signature pastry, and a coffee before settling in for a tan and a swim. Since the island is popular with Neapolitan day-trippers and summer residents (mostly from Naples), bakeries are constantly baking off these fresh pastries with rounded edges named for their shape—*lingua* means "tongue" in Italian.

In a medium saucepan, whisk together the egg yolks, sugar, corn starch, salt, milk, and lemon zest. Heat the mixture over medium heat, whisking constantly, until it simmers, about 4 minutes. Lift the saucepan occasionally to diffuse the heat and prevent scalding. Simmer, whisking constantly, until the cream thickens, about 1 minute more. The whisk should leave a trail in the cream.

Transfer the mixture to a medium bowl and cover with plastic wrap so the plastic touches the surface of the cream. This will prevent a skin from forming. Set the bowl in a larger bowl filled with ice water. Cool the cream completely.

Meanwhile, preheat the oven to 400°F. Line a baking sheet with parchment paper.

Roll out the puff pastry into a rectangle that is approximately 10 × 20 inches and less than ⅛ inch thick. Using a knife, cut the dough into 20 rectangles measuring 5 × 2 inches each. Lay 10 of the rectangles on the prepared baking sheet, leaving about ¼ inch between each.

Spoon the cream onto the rectangles, distributing it evenly and keeping the cream in the middle, ½ inch away from each edge. Cover each with one of the remaining 10 rectangles and seal the edges with water. Using a sharp knife or pastry cutter, round off the edges so the pastries are shaped like elongated ovals. Brush the top of each pastry with egg white, sprinkle with sugar, and bake until golden, about 20 minutes. Serve immediately or allow to cool to room temperature and store in an airtight container for up to 2 days.

Puff Pastry

Makes 1 pound (about ½ kilogram) puff pastry

250 grams (2 cups) all-purpose flour, plus more for
    dusting

3 grams (½ teaspoon) sea salt

250 grams (1 cup plus 2 tablespoons) cold unsalted
    butter, cut into ½-inch pieces

125 milliliters (½ cup) ice-cold water

Sift the flour and salt onto a work surface and make a
well in the middle. Add the butter to the well and work
it into the flour by hand, squeezing the pieces flat as
you go. Continue to mix quickly and lightly with your
fingertips until the butter is grainy and flour-covered.

Sprinkle half the ice water over the flour mixture and
gather the dough into a ball. Add additional water by
the tablespoon until a shaggy dough, neither sticky nor
shiny, forms. (You may not need all the water.)

Wrap the dough in plastic wrap and chill in the
refrigerator for 30 minutes.

Remove the dough from the refrigerator. On a lightly
floured surface, working in only one direction, roll
the dough into a rectangle that is approximately
10 × 5 inches and ⅛ inch thick.

With one short edge facing you, fold the top third
farthest from you toward the middle, then the bottom
third over that like a letter. Turn the dough clockwise
a quarter turn, so that the open fold is now facing you.
Roll this dough again into a 10 × 5-inch rectangle and
repeat the folds. Wrap the dough in plastic wrap and
chill in the refrigerator for 30 minutes.

Repeat the rolling-and-turning process once more and
allow the dough to chill for at least 30 minutes in the
refrigerator before using. It will keep, wrapped tightly
in plastic wrap, in the refrigerator for up to 3 days or
in the freezer for up to 4 weeks.

MULIGNANA
C'A'
CIUCCULATA

Fried Eggplant Smothered
in Chocolate

Serves 4 to 6

Neutral oil (see page 37) or olive oil,
for frying

3 slender eggplants, peeled and sliced
crosswise into ¼-inch-thick slices

1 cup all-purpose flour

Sea salt

1½ cups heavy cream

6 ounces dark chocolate, roughly
chopped (about 1 cup)

2 tablespoons *concerto* or Liquore
Strega

¼ cup candied orange zest, cut into
¼-inch pieces

¼ cup roughly chopped almonds

Maldon salt to finish

NOTE The flavor of eggplants
develops throughout their growing
season. Young eggplant shouldn't
require salting, but later on, they may
develop a bitter flavor. Salting reduces
bitterness and improves texture. Lay the
eggplant slices in a colander or on a wire
rack over the sink, sprinkle with salt,
and place a heavy plate on top. Allow to
rest for about an hour before rinsing.

Maori, home to the Amalfi Coast's longest sand beach,
is flanked by watchtowers that once defended the town
against invasions from the sea. In the eighth century,
Arab invaders conquered the town, bringing with them
what were at the time exotic ingredients like eggplants
(see page 159), which now dominate local menus, even
appearing in sweets. Each year around Ferragosto,
the mid-August holiday celebrating the Assumption
of the Virgin, Maori residents gather around tables to
enjoy *mulignana c'a' ciucculata*, fried eggplant drenched
in spiced melted chocolate and studded with candied
fruits and nuts. Although locals claim the dish is almost
a thousand years old, chocolate didn't arrive in the
area until after the discovery of the New World—
the Spanish who controlled Campania until 1861
introduced bitter chocolate to the region—so its age is
likely only a century or two. Some cooks use an herb-
infused liqueur called *concerto* in the dish. The liqueur
comes from the Tramonti convent near Maori, but you
can replace it with grappa or Strega.

In a medium frying pan or cast-iron skillet, heat 2 inches
of oil to 350°F. Line a wire rack with paper towels.

Place the flour in a shallow medium bowl. Dip each slice
of eggplant in flour, shaking off any excess. Add the
eggplant to the hot oil, working in batches as needed,
and fry until golden brown. Transfer to the lined rack to
drain and immediately season with sea salt.

In a medium saucepan, heat the cream over low heat,
stirring to prevent scalding, until very hot and steaming
but not boiling. Place the chocolate in a large bowl. Pour
the cream over the chocolate and allow it to sit for
about 2 minutes to melt the chocolate, then stir until
smooth and well combined. Stir in the *concerto*. Set
aside to cool completely, about 20 minutes.

Dip the eggplant into the chocolate, allowing excess to
drip off, and place in a medium baking dish until one layer
is complete. Sprinkle orange zest and almonds over the
layer. Repeat until the eggplant and toppings have been
used, ending with chocolate. Chill in the refrigerator for
at least 2 hours. Slice into rectangles and serve with
Maldon salt.

LIQUORI E COCKTAIL

—

LIQUEURS AND COCKTAILS

LIMONCELLO

Citrus Liqueur

Makes 8 cups

4 cups (1 liter) Everclear (190 proof)

Zest of 5 untreated organic lemons, removed with a vegetable peeler (I like *femminello di Santa Teresa*, *sfusato amalfitano*, or Meyer lemons)

5 untreated organic lemons

60 fresh bay leaves, washed and crushed

4 cups water

5 cups sugar

Limoncello is a popular digestif from Campania's Amalfi Coast, where terraced citrus groves cascade through valleys nearly to the edge of the Tyrrhenian Sea. There, varieties of lemons like *femminello di Santa Teresa* and *sfusato amalfitano* are particularly prized, and their skins are rich in fragrant essential oils, giving *limoncello* its distinct aroma and citrus flavor. The procedure for making *limoncello* doesn't change much from one home to another: lemon zest is infused in alcohol, rested, then sweetened with rich simple syrup. This traditional method is good enough, but for a slightly cleaner final product, I prefer Franny's recipe. This now defunct Brooklyn-based Italophile restaurant made *limoncello* by suspending lemons in cheesecloth over vodka, allowing it to absorb the citrus aromas by osmosis. They finished it with a bit of zest in the vodka. This version is a blend of the Sorrento- and Brooklyn-styles, which uses the suspension method with the traditional Everclear rather than vodka. *Limoncello* takes about five weeks to prepare.

Place the alcohol and lemon zest in a large glass jar. Using cheesecloth, suspend the whole lemons in the jar above the alcohol, taking care not to let them touch the liquid. Seal the jar and let rest in a cool, dark place for 30 days. Agitate the jar every few days.

On the last day, combine the water and sugar in a large saucepan and heat over medium-high heat. Meanwhile, strain the infused alcohol into a clean jar, discarding the zest and lemons. When the sugar has dissolved, 3 to 5 minutes, remove the pan from the heat and allow the syrup to cool, about 20 minutes.

Add three-quarters of the syrup to the jar with the alcohol. Taste and adjust the sweetness, adding more syrup as needed. Seal the jar and allow the liquid to rest in a dark place at room temperature for 1 week.

Serve very cold or over ice. The *limoncello* will keep in a sealed container in the refrigerator for at least 6 months and in the freezer for well over a year. (Due to the high alcohol content, the liquid will not freeze.)

NOTE Since the lemon zest is the main flavoring ingredient here, only use untreated organic lemons. You can substitute mandarins, bitter oranges, or any other citrus for the lemons—just be sure they're organic and untreated, too.

NEGRONI _DEL_ CAPO

Makes 1 drink

1 ounce London dry gin

1 ounce sweet vermouth

¾ ounce Vecchio Amaro del Capo

1 lemon wheel

The Negroni, a classic Italian cocktail composed of equal parts gin, Campari, and sweet vermouth, was first mixed for Count Camillo Negroni at Florence's Cafè Casoni in 1919. This variation adopts the flavors of the south, swapping out the Campari for Vecchio Amaro del Capo, an herbal infusion made in Calabria's Capo Vaticano, and changes the liquor ratio, scaling back the bitter component for greater balance.

Pour the gin, vermouth, and amaro into a tumbler with ice. Stir and garnish with the lemon.

FINOCCHIELLO

Wild Fennel Liqueur

Makes 8 cups

4 cups (1 liter) Everclear (190 Proof)

1 bunch wild fennel, washed and torn

2 teaspoons crushed fennel seeds

4 cups water

5 cups sugar

This wild fennel liqueur recipe is versatile and is the basis for all sorts of other herbal liqueurs made in the lush Apennine region spanning Molise, Campania, and Basilicata. Herbal digestifs take about five weeks to make, so they require some patience, but they are super simple and, thanks to their high alcohol content, last for ages. Traditional, herbal liqueurs are served after meals, but you could mix them with soda water and serve as a cocktail, if you wish.

Place the alcohol, wild fennel, and fennel seeds in a large glass jar. Seal and keep in a cool, dark place for 30 days. Agitate the jar every few days.

On the last day, combine the water and sugar in a large saucepan and heat over medium-high heat. Meanwhile, strain the infused alcohol into a clean jar, discarding the wild fennel and fennel seeds. When the sugar has dissolved, 3 to 5 minutes, remove the pan from the heat and allow the syrup to cool, about 20 minutes.

Add three-quarters of the syrup to the jar with the alcohol. Taste and adjust the sweetness, adding more syrup as needed. Seal the jar and allow the liquid to rest in a dark place at room temperature for 1 week.

Serve very cold or over ice. The digestif will keep in a sealed container in the refrigerator for at least 6 months and in the freezer for well over a year. (Due to the high alcohol content, the liquid will not freeze.)

Amaro is a genre of bitter-sweet infused liquors made by steeping fruits, spices, flowers, and medicinal herbs in spirit. The result is a bitter concoction, which is sweetened with syrup and tinted with caramel coloring to turn it a shade of brown. Throughout Italy, but particularly in the south, *amari* are sipped after meals and praised for their digestive benefits.

Homemade herbal liquors like *Finocchiello* (page 234) are still fairly common throughout the south, but *amari* are often made from numerous obscure foraged ingredients and are almost always produced in proper distilleries by large industrial brands. One such brand, Distilleria Caffo, makes *amari* as well as digestifs flavored with anise, *finocchietto selvatico* (wild fennel), bergamot, prickly pears, and *mirto* (wild myrtle). The distillery, now in its fourth generation of family ownership, was founded in the 1890s when Giuseppe Caffo started distilling grappa from grape pressings from Mount Etna in Sicily. Eventually, his sons bought a distillery on the mainland in Limbadi, Calabria. The family business still has its home base there but has now expanded to Udine, near where Italy borders Slovenia, and to Germany in order to satisfy the growing global demand.

Caffo's flagship product, Vecchio Amaro del Capo, takes its name from Capo Vaticano, a wide cape midway down Calabria's craggy Tyrrhenian coast. The label features a naïve art–style rendering of the seaside and prickly pears, rooting it clearly in its place of origin. Amaro del Capo is made with a proprietary blend of ingredients, including mandarin, star anise, chamomile, juniper, licorice, mint, and hyssop, all of which are plucked from Calabrian soil. The infused spirit is diluted to 70 proof after the addition of sugar and water. The squat, square bottle is stored in freezers all over the south, where the bitter and sweet digestif is poured to signal the end of a meal.

Across the border in Basilicata, another family distillery dutifully makes traditional *amari* based on historic recipes. Founded by baker Pasquale Vena in 1894, Amaro Lucano was so highly prized that Italy's royal family proclaimed Vena as its official amaro maker—the monarch's coat of arms on the label is proof. As a young boy, Vena dreamed of going to America but only made it as far as Naples, where he became acquainted with medicinal herbs while studying pastry making. He returned home, opened his own bakery, and experimented with various infusions in the back room, ultimately inventing Amaro Lucano, a blend of thirty herbs and fruits. The company is now run by Vena's grandchildren and great-grandchildren who evangelize amaro's bitter-sweet flavor profile across the globe.

In neighboring Puglia, Amaro Margapoti, a small family-run amaro operation, started in Gallipoli in 2001. Angela Margapoti and her parents, Fernando and Antonietta, have adapted a century-old family recipe and now sell their artisanal amaro and other infusions, which they bottle in their apartment near the Ionian Sea. They macerate china, cloves, cinnamon, and other spices to create tinctures, which they dilute in antique 5-liter demijohn bottles. The process is certainly small scale and hands on, hearkening back to the methods of the distant past—the same ones used by Giuseppe Caffo and Pasquale Vena when they were launching their own companies more than a century ago.

AMARO

Bitter Digestif

Makes 8 cups

4 cups (1 liter) Everclear (190 proof)

1 teaspoon juniper berries

1 teaspoon dried oregano

1 teaspoon ground angelica root

1 teaspoon ground gentian

1 teaspoon crushed black peppercorns

1 sprig fresh rosemary

1 tablespoon dried chamomile flowers

Zest of 1 bitter orange, removed with a vegetable peeler

Zest of 1 lemon, removed with a vegetable peeler

2 bay leaves

4 cups water

5 cups sugar

This amaro recipe comes from deep in the Apennines, where shepherds make it from foraged herbs and roots. Amaro takes about five weeks to prepare.

Place the alcohol, juniper berries, oregano, angelica root, gentian, peppercorns, rosemary, chamomile flowers, citrus zests, and bay leaves in a large glass jar. Seal and keep in a dark place for 30 days. Agitate the jar every few days.

On the last day, combine the water and sugar in a large saucepan and heat over medium-high heat. Meanwhile, strain the infused alcohol into a clean jar, discarding the herbs and spices. When the sugar has dissolved, 3 to 5 minutes, remove the pan from the heat and allow the syrup to cool, about 20 minutes.

Add three-quarters of the syrup to the jar with the alcohol. Taste and adjust the sweetness, adding more syrup as needed. Seal the jar and allow the liquid to rest in a dark place at room temperature for 1 week.

Serve very cold or over ice. The digestif will keep in a sealed container in the refrigerator for at least 6 months and in the freezer for well over a year. (Due to the high alcohol content, the liquid will not freeze.)

RATAFIÀ

Cherry Vermouth

Makes 5½ cups

1⅓ pounds sour cherries, pitted

1 (750 milliliters) bottle dry red wine
 (I like Aglianico del Vulture)

2 cinnamon sticks

1 tablespoon freshly ground coffee
 beans

1 cup water

1 cup sugar

⅔ cup Everclear (190 proof)

This sweet and fruity vermouth is enjoyed as a postprandial liqueur throughout the lower Apennines. Whole *visciole* (sour cherries) are harvested in the spring, steeped in structured red wine like Montepulciano d'Abruzzo or Aglianico del Vulture, fortified with spirit, and sweetened with syrup. Use wild sour cherries, available in the late spring and early summer, if you can, but you can use sweet conventional cherries instead, though bear in mind that you may have to adjust the syrup accordingly. *Ratafià* takes about five weeks to prepare.

Place the cherries, wine, cinnamon sticks, and coffee in a large glass jar. Seal and keep in a sunny place for 30 days. Agitate the jar every few days.

On the last day, combine the water and sugar in a large saucepan and heat over medium-high heat. Meanwhile, strain the infused wine into a clean jar, discarding the cherries, cinnamon, and coffee. When the sugar has dissolved, 3 to 5 minutes, remove the pan from the heat and allow the syrup to cool, about 20 minutes.

Add the alcohol and three-quarters of the syrup to the jar (start with just half the syrup if using sweet cherries). Taste and adjust the sweetness, adding more syrup as needed. Seal the jar and allow the liquid to rest in a dark place at room temperature for 1 week.

Serve very cold or over ice. *Ratafià* will keep in a sealed container in the refrigerator for at least 2 months and in the freezer for about 6 months. (Due to the high alcohol content, the liquid will not freeze.)

WITCH ON THE BEACH

Makes 1 drink

1½ ounces London dry gin

½ ounce Liquore Strega

½ ounce fresh lemon juice

½ ounce Rich Simple Syrup
(recipe follows)

Pulp from ½ passion fruit

Splash of soda water

Lemon twist

Sprig of fresh mint

Italy's blossoming craft cocktail movement was born in Milan a little over a decade ago and has been slow to spread to the south, where anything more complicated than a spritz or more exotic than a mojito is tough to find. The major exception is at Quanto Basta, a craft cocktail bar in the historic center of Lecce, where Italian and imported spirits mingle. In his Witch on the Beach, mixologist Mauro Urro stirs together herbaceous gin with saffron-infused Liquore Strega (see page 242) in this modified gin sour.

Pour the gin, Strega, lemon juice, simple syrup, and passion fruit into a tumbler with ice. Stir and top with a splash of soda water. Garnish with the lemon twist and sprig of fresh mint.

Rich Simple Syrup
Makes 1 cup rich simple syrup

2 cups sugar   1 cup water

In a small saucepan, combine the sugar and water. Heat over medium-high heat, stirring, until the sugar has dissolved, 3 to 5 minutes.

Remove from the heat and set aside to cool, about 15 minutes. Store in a sealed jar in the refrigerator for up to 2 weeks.

Liquore Strega
Strega

Just one year before the Spanish were defeated and the south came under the rule of the newly unified Italian state, Carmine Vincenzo Alberti and Giuseppe Alberti, father and son, created Liquore Strega in Benevento. Since 1860, the Alberti family has produced this herbal infusion that features more than seventy ingredients, including mint, cinnamon, iris, nutmeg, juniper, and saffron, which gives the liquid its highlighter-yellow hue.

There's a bottle of the stuff in practically every household in the south—and quite a few Italian American home bars, as well—and unlike amaro (see page 236) and *Limoncello* (page 233), Strega has found a place for itself outside the realm of digestive liqueurs, often appearing in cookie and cake recipes like *Pigna di Pasqua* (page 217), an Easter cake from the Sannio subregion of Campania.

The word *strega* means "witch," a reference to the superstition that surrounds the city of the liqueur's origin. According to local folklore, Benevento has been the meeting place of witches since the Lombards conquered the city in the seventh century. Although they were Christian converts, the Lombards incorporated elements of their ancient pagan religion into their new beliefs. Stories of witches gathering under walnut trees—a scene of which is depicted on Strega's art nouveau–style label—were popular in the Middle Ages. In successive centuries, this quaint

legend took on a sinister character as the Catholic Church conducted witch-hunts and trials, many of which resulted in the execution of suspected witches.

Today, *beneventani* are proud of their superstition—it's not unusual for a local to report the legend of witches as though it were verifiable history—and of their local liqueur, a savory concoction that has been made in the same distillery building near the Benevento train station since the Albertis invented the potent brew almost 160 years ago.

LIQUORE ALLA LIQUIRIZIA

Licorice Liqueur

Makes 9 cups

3½ ounces pure licorice (I like Amarelli)

5 cups water

4 cups (1 liter) Everclear (190 proof)

5½ cups sugar

From its famous Tropea onions to its piquant chile peppers, Calabria is a region known for its bold, strong flavors. It's almost as though its soil demands intensity. It should be no surprise, then, that Italy's most prestigious licorice roots grow in the region. The Amarelli family has been making licorice in Rossano since 1731—their museum in the town details the production process and the history of one of Italy's oldest family businesses—and it is used for, among other things, this after-dinner drink. *Liquore alla liquirizia* takes about two weeks to prepare.

Place the licorice in a large glass jar and cover with 1 cup of the water. Seal and keep in a cool, dark place until the licorice breaks down, about 3 days. Agitate the jar twice a day.

On the third day, pour the Everclear into the bottle with the licorice. In a large saucepan, heat the remaining 4 cups water and sugar together over medium-high heat. When the sugar has dissolved, 3 to 5 minutes, remove the pan from the heat and allow the syrup to cool, about 20 minutes.

Add three-quarters of the syrup to the jar with the licorice and alcohol. Taste and adjust the sweetness, adding more syrup as needed. Seal the jar and allow the liquid to rest in a dark place at room temperature for 1 week.

Serve very cold or over ice. The digestif will keep in a sealed container in the refrigerator for at least 6 months and in the freezer for well over a year. (Due to the high alcohol content, the liquid will not freeze.)

NUCILLO

Walnut Liqueur

Makes 5 cups

4 cups (1 liter) Everclear (190 proof)

24 green walnuts, halved

2 cinnamon sticks

5 whole cloves

½ teaspoon freshly grated nutmeg

1 cup water

1¾ cups sugar

Around Naples, Benevento, and Caserta, local tradition dictates that *nucillo* must be made from green walnuts harvested on June 24, the Feast of San Giovanni Battista, and steeped in alcohol for forty days. Throughout the zone, pharmacists would sell *cuoncio d'o nucillo*, a proprietary mix of spices used to flavor *nucillo*. The homemade *nucillo* tradition is now verging on extinction, and pharmacies have shifted their offerings away from digestif ingredients to cellulite cream and beauty products. Only Dr. Vincenzo Tortora still makes his own *cuoncio*, a mix of china, cinnamon, cloves, and nutmeg, each chosen for its balancing flavor and medicinal use: pain relief (nutmeg), muscle spasms (cinnamon), and stomach issues (china).

The June 24 walnut harvest date isn't random. The Feast of San Giovanni Battista is on the same day as the reputed witch rituals in Benevento (see page 242). Witches would gather around a walnut tree, brew a potent elixir, and share it with engaged couples.

To try *nucillo* before diving into the process, look for 'E Curti brand. *Nucillo* takes about two months to prepare.

Place the alcohol and walnuts in a large glass jar. Seal and keep in a warm, dark place for 40 days. Agitate the jar every few days.

On the last day, strain the infused alcohol into a separate jar and discard the walnuts or use them to make *Nocillato* (recipe follows). Add the cinnamon, cloves, and nutmeg, seal the jar, and keep in a warm, dark place for 20 days.

On the last day, combine the water and sugar in a large saucepan and heat over medium-high heat. Meanwhile, strain the infused alcohol into a clean jar, discarding the spices. When the sugar has dissolved, 3 to 5 minutes, remove the pan from the heat and allow the syrup to cool, about 20 minutes.

Add three-quarters of the syrup to the jar with the alcohol. Taste and adjust the sweetness, adding more syrup as needed. Seal the jar and allow the liquid to rest in a dark place at room temperature for 1 week.

Serve chilled. The *nucillo* will keep in a sealed container in the refrigerator for at least 6 months and in the freezer for about a year. (Due to the high alcohol content, the liquid will not freeze.)

Nocillato

After you filter out the alcohol-infused walnuts from *nucillo*, use them to make a sort of Campanian vermouth by steeping the boozy nuts in red wine.

24 green walnuts, discarded from *nucillo* production (see page 244)

1 (750-milliliters) bottle dry red wine (I like Piedirosso)

Place the walnuts and wine in a large glass jar. Seal and keep in a warm, dark place for 1 week. Agitate the jar once a day.

Serve chilled. The *nocillato* will keep in a sealed container in the refrigerator for at least 4 weeks and in the freezer for about 6 months. (Due to the high alcohol content, the liquid will not freeze.)

ACKNOWLEDGMENTS

Thanks to my mom, Joj, and my dad, Papa Parla, who accompanied me on more than a few South Italy journeys. Thank you to Hans Fama, who fed and nurtured me during the editing process. The whole Clarkson Potter and Crown Publishing team has given me the most wonderful support. *Grazie* Maya Mavjee, Aaron Wehner, Doris Cooper, Kate Tyler, Carly Gorga, Stephanie Davis, Jana Branson, Stephanie Huntwork, Ian Dingman, Terry Deal, Linnea Knollmueller, and Gabrielle Van Tassel. To my editor, Amanda Englander, fellow Jersey native and pizza lover, I am so grateful for the constant encouragement, friendship, and texts featuring a resplendent basset hound.

Ed Anderson, my fearless photographer and travel companion, I am so glad we survived our road trip (no thanks to my driving) and thank you for introducing me to the supremely kind and talented George Dolese, whose styling and sourcing skills brought the recipes of South Italy to life.

John Regefalk, my dear friend and tireless dough developer, I am so grateful for your friendship and dedication. Your doughs are amazing. Move back to Rome, *per favore?* Props to Noel Brohner for baking off a beautiful Matera bread. Dajjjeee Cesare Agostini, *maestro delle friselle.*

Grazie to my pals Chris Behr and Sara Levi at the Rome Sustainable Food Project for their insight, recipe development, and support—not to mention access to their cookbook library.

My friend and recipe tester Tatiana Perea is a force of nature. *Gracias, amiga.* Thanks also to Dave Potes for his feedback and testing.

This book was a team effort and would not have been possible without the generosity of countless food and beverage producers who selflessly opened their kitchens, bakeries, and homes and donated their time, resources, and recipes. Infinite thanks and respect go out: Angela, Vincenzo, and Roberto at 'E Curti; Angelica, Annarita, and Rinaldo at Regio Tratturo; Carmela Bruno and Ali Coccaro at La Piazzetta; Armando Romito and Maestri del Sannio; Lucia Parente; Giuditta Gianfrancesco; la famiglia Masella; Molino Mirra; Franco Pepe; la famiglia Tortora; Le Campestre; La Sbecciatrice; Museo Etnico Arbëreshë Civita; Alberto Bloise; La Locanda di Alia; La Grotta di Zi' Concetta; Giuseppe and Zio Gaetano Di Martino; Caseificio Vannulo; Angelo and Nicola Romano; Franca Cozzolino; Giuseppe Gatto and Lucrezia Galia; la famiglia Margapoti; Enzo Bruno and the Cooperativa Padre Pio; Simona, Mino, and Antonio Rosati and Elisabetta Scaraglio; Angelo and Vito Dicessa, Giuseppe and Giuseppe Di Gesù; Angela, Antonella, and Peppe De Marco; Domenico Tortorella, Carlo Abate, Matteo, Pasquale, and Lorenzo; Donatella Marino and Alici di Menaica; Giulio Giordano and Nettuno; i ragazzi di Quanto Basta.

Costantino, Rosetta with Janet Fletcher. *My Calabria: Rustic Family Cooking from Italy's Undiscovered South*. New York: W. W. Norton & Company, 2010.

Levi, Carlo. *Christ Stopped at Eboli*. New York: FSG Classics, 2006.

Mallo, Beppe. *Calabria e Lucania in Bocca*. Palermo: Il Vespro, 1979.

Murphy, Trevor. *Pliny the Elder's Natural History: The Empire in the Encyclopedia*. Oxford, UK: Oxford University Press, 2004.

Riley, Gillian. *The Oxford Companion to Italian Food*. Oxford, UK: Oxford University Press, 2009.

Sada, Luigi. *Puglie in Bocca*. Palermo: Il Vespro, 1979.

Zanini De Vita, Oretta. *Encyclopedia of Pasta*. Translated by Mauren Fant. Oakland, CA: University of California Press, 2009.

Food

Anson Mills
803-467-4122
ansonmills.com
For organic heirloom wheat flours.

Bluebird Grain Farms
509-996-3526
bluebirdgrainfarms.com
For quality grains milled to order.

Boccalone
415-433-6500
boccalone.com
For *guanciale, lardo,* and *'nduja.*

Buon'Italia
212-633-9090
buonitalia.com
For flours, pasta, salted anchovies, cheese, *guanciale,* and assorted Italian specialties.

Caputo Brothers Creamery
717-739-1091
caputobrotherscreamery.com
For mozzarella, ricotta, provolone, and *ricotta salata* made in southwestern Pennsylvania. They also sell cultured mozzarella curds in case you want to try making your own.

Di Bruno Brothers
215-531-5666
dibruno.com
For Pecorino Romano, Parmigiano-Reggiano, Gorgonzola, sheep's-milk ricotta, mozzarella, and other Italian cheese, as well as *guanciale.*

Formaggio Kitchen
888-212-3224
formaggiokitchen.com

For *guanciale,* cheeses, pastas, olive oils, and other specialty products.

Gioia Cheese Co.
626-444-6015
gioiacheeseco.com
This Southern California–based family-owned company produces mozzarella, ricotta, and *burrata.*

Gustiamo
718-860-2949
gustiamo.com
This online retailer stocks Italy's finest *colatura,* salted anchovies, tomato sauces, and more.

King Arthur Flour
800-827-6836
kingarthurflour.com
For quality flours.

La Quercia
515-981-1625
laquercia.us
For cured meats and salami like *'nduja.*

Local Harvest
831-515-5602
localharvest.org
A network of local farms for sourcing fresh pork jowl for *guanciale,* among other things.

Market Hall Foods
510-250-6006
markethallfoods.com
For fennel pollen, salted anchovies, colatura, durum wheat pasta, and a wide range of Italian specialty products.

Murray's Cheese
888-692-4339
murrayscheese.com
For *guanciale, 'nduja,* cheeses, and Italian specialty products of all kinds.

'Nduja Artisans
312-550-6991
ndujaartisans.com
The premier domestic producer of spicy Calabrian *salumi.*

Rancho Gordo
707-259-1935
ranchogordo.com
For borlotti (cranberry beans).

Salumeria Biellese
salumeriabiellese.com
For *guanciale* and *'nduja.*

Zingerman's
888-636-8162
zingermans.com
For *guanciale, lardo, 'nduja,* cheeses, *peperoni cruschi,* and a huge variety of Italian specialty products.

Utensils

JB Prince
212-683-3553
jbprince.com
Baking sheets, terrine molds, baking utensils, and kitchen equipment.

OXO
oxo.com
800-545-4411
Good, sturdy cooking and baking utensils.

Sur La Table
800-243-0852
surlatable.com
High-end cookwear, sturdy pots, and pizza stones.

Williams-Sonoma
877-812-6235
williams-sonoma.com
For cookware, bakeware, baking stones, cocktail tools, ice cream makers, ice cube trays, and assorted baking tools.

CONVERSIONS

Weight

US	Metric
½ ounce	14.2 grams
1 ounce	28.3 grams
1 pound (16 ounces)	453 grams
2.2 pounds	1 kilogram

Some sample weights

	Measure	Weight (grams)
All-purpose flour	1 cup	about 125 grams
Bread flour	1 cup	about 140 grams
Extra-virgin olive oil	1 tablespoon	about 14 grams
Salt	1 teaspoon	about 6 grams
Granulated sugar	1 cup	about 200 grams
Grated Parmigiano-Reggiano	1 ounce	28.3 grams
Grated Pecorino Romano	1 ounce	28.3 grams

Liquid volume

1 teaspoon = 4.9 milliliters
1 tablespoon = 3 teaspoons = 14.7 milliliters
1 cup = 237 milliliters
4.22 cups = 1 liter

Length

1 inch = 2.5 centimeters
1 centimeter = .4 inches

Published in the United States by
Clarkson Potter/Publishers, an imprint of
the Crown Publishing Group, a division of
Penguin Random House LLC, New York.
crownpublishing.com
clarksonpotter.com

CLARKSON POTTER is a trademark
and POTTER with colophon is a
registered trademark of Penguin Random
House LLC.

Library of Congress Cataloging-in-
Publication Data
Title: Flavors of the Italian south: tastes
and traditions from Campania to Calabria
/ Katie Parla.
Description: First edition. | New York
: Clarkson Potter/Publishers. [2019] |
Includes bibliographical references
and index.

Identifiers: LCCN 2018020557 (print) |
LCCN 2018022239 (ebook) | ISBN
9781524760472 (ebook) | ISBN
9781524760465 (hardcover)
Subjects: LCSH: Cooking, Italian—
Southern style. | LCGFT: Cookbooks.
Classification: LCC TX723.2.S65 (ebook) |
LCC TX723.2.S65 P37 2019 (print) |
DDC 641.5945—dc23
LC record available at https://lccn.loc.gov/
2018020557

ISBN 978-1-5247-6046-5
Ebook 978-1-5247-6047-2

Printed in China

Book and cover design by Ian Dingman
Cover photographs by Ed Anderson
Photographs on pages 11 and 125 by
Katie Parla.

10 9 8 7 6 5 4 3 2 1

First Edition

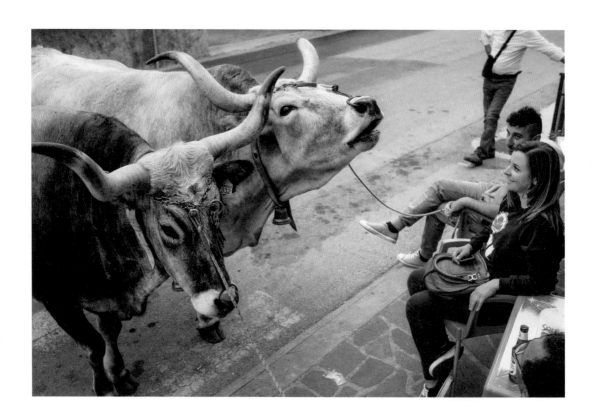

FOR MY FATHER